Evaluating the Evaluators

Maurice Holt

HODDER AND STOUGHTON

LONDON SYDNEY AUCKLAND TORONTO

British Library Cataloguing in Publication Data

Holt, Maurice
    Evaluating the evaluators. — (Studies in teaching and learning)
    1. Educational surveys
    I. Title   II. Series
    379.1'5   LB2823

ISBN 0 340 27245 7   Paperback

First published 1981

Typeset by Graphic Consultants International Ltd, Singapore.
Printed and bound in Great Britain for
Hodder and Stoughton Educational,
a division of Hodder and Stoughton Ltd,
Mill Road, Dunton Green, Sevenoaks, Kent,
by Richard Clay (The Chaucer Press) Ltd, Bungay, Suffolk.

Evaluating the Evaluators

Studies in Teaching and Learning
General Editor
Denis Lawton, B.A., Ph.D.
Professor of Education and Deputy Director,
University of London Institute of Education

In the series:

Denis Lawton *An Introduction to Teaching and Learning*
John Roberston *Effective Classroom Control*
Maurice Holt *Evaluating the Evaluators*
Richard Aldrich *An Introduction to the History of Education*
Denis Lawton *Curriculum Studies and Educational Planning*
Richard Pring *Personal and Social Development*

Contents

Studies in Teaching and Learning

The purpose of this series of short books on education is to make available readable, up-to-date views on educational issues and controversies. Its aim will be to provide teachers and students (and perhaps parents and governors) with a series of books which will introduce those educational topics which any intelligent and professional educationist ought to be familiar with. One of the criticisms levelled against 'teacher-education' is that there is so little agreement about what ground should be covered in courses at various levels; one assumption behind this series of texts is that there is a common core of knowledge and skills that all teachers need to be aware of, and the series is designed to map out this territory.

Although the major intention of the series is to provide general coverage, each volume will consist of more than a review of the relevant literature; the individual authors will be encouraged to give their own personal interpretation of the field and the way it is developing.

In this book, for simplicity of style, 'he' has been taken to subsume 'she'.

Preface

A central argument of this book is that evaluation in education, like any kind of social research, cannot be value-free. An evaluator, like a researcher, has to choose; to choose which data, which interviews, which interpretation. Evaluation is therefore a political activity, since political questions arise when people disagree and a choice has to be made.

It follows that any evaluator is biased, and this is true of one who, as in my case, sets out to evaluate the evaluators. If the reader is to reach his own interpretation of my arguments, he needs to know something of my own prejudices.

In the main, these are bound to emerge from the text itself. To argue that an evaluation can take up a neutral stance, and leave someone else to take the decisions, seems to me an unsustainable position; a more defensible procedure is to make one's own views clear and expose them to the evaluation of others. But it may be helpful for the reader to know how I come to make this evaluation: to know what sort of experiences prompt me to set out these arguments.

My own view is that an over-emphasis on the need for evaluation, as one of the processes in curriculum design, development and implementation, will not of itself help teachers improve the schools they work in. And this feeling derives from my own experience as a teacher, a head of department, a deputy head and a headmaster. In the latter case, as head of Sheredes School, Hertfordshire, I spent eight years with a team of dedicated staff developing a common 11-16 curriculum for all pupils in an 11-18 mixed comprehensive school, and this substantial essay in school-based whole curriculum planning has had a decisive influence on my thinking (Holt, 1978, 1979). Since this kind of curriculum development is now widely regarded as a desirable activity for schools, I am inclined to think my own conclusions may be helpful.

Subsequently, in my work as an education and curriculum consultant, I have been associated with the process of curriculum change in a number of schools. And while an evaluation of each school's work has played some part in this process, the decisive influence has seemed to me to be a careful reflection upon the educational principles which govern the way in which teachers initiate their activities.

Furthermore, in the course of making this study of formal assessment in education, I have come to the view that an emphasis on evaluation as an explicit and separate activity in a variety of modes and forms may be confusing, rather than clarifying, to teachers whose prime concern is with curriculum change. Yet most evaluation exercises have in common a desire to bring about curriculum change. As I have come to see the considerable innate difficulties of making a formal evaluation of any educational process or outcome, so my misgivings have grown. A good school will certainly make use of processes of evaluation; but making use of processes of evaluation may not alone produce a good school. There may be national testing, and local authority assessments, in a variety of forms and subjects; and a school may practise elaborate forms of self audit, but unless its curriculum thinking is sound, it may still be an unsatisfactory school.

This personal note is offered in the hope that it will allow the reader to determine my own value stance, and so make a better interpretation of the account and argument which follow.

Acknowledgments

Many people have been good enough to give up their time to talk to me about their opinions and experiences of evaluation, and I should like to name them all. Alas, the political nature of educational evaluation makes this a risky business, and most of them must remain anonymous. I hope, therefore, that all the teachers, advisers, inspectors and officers who gave me their help — on and off the record — will accept this expression of thanks for their kindness. I hope, too, that they will feel I have been able to do some justice to their views and that, as a result, this book helps to throw light on some important issues which need wider discussion.

I am grateful to Professor Harvey Goldstein and Dr Robert Wood of the University of London Institute of Education, whose research project 'The Evaluation of Testing in Schools' will investigate part of my subject much more closely than I, and who were most generous in enlightening me on the intricacies of testing. Needless to say, any errors in my account arise from my own misunderstandings. I must thank, too, Helen Simons and Jeanette Williams for so willingly sharing their specialist knowledge with me. Henry Macintosh, Secretary of the Southern Regional Examinations Board, was kind enough to talk to me about styles of public examination and their connection with school assessment.

I owe a particular debt to Professor Richard Pring, of the University of Exeter, for his guidance and encouragement, and for making some American documents available to me; and to Michael Golby, also of the University of Exeter, whose perception and understanding were invaluable.

My special thanks must go to Professor Denis Lawton, Deputy Director of the University of London Institute of Education, who first suggested that I write this book, and whose advice and insight have been of the greatest help to me.

January 1981   Cullompton, Devon

Abbreviations

APU	Assessment of Performance Unit (of DES)
CED	Centre for Educational Disadvantage
CEO	Chief Education Officer (of an LEA)
CNAA	Council for National Academic Awards
COG	Coordinating Group (of the APU)
CON	Consultative Committee (of the APU)
CSE	Certificate of Secondary Education
CSSE	Case Studies in Science Education (US)
DES	Department of Education and Science
ECS	Education Commission of the States (US)
EEC	European Economic Community
GCE	General Certificate of Education
HEW	Department of Health, Education and Welfare (US)
HMI	Her Majesty's Inspectorate/Inspector (of schools)
ILEA	Inner London Education Authority
ILIS	Independent Learning in Science Project
LEA	Local Education Authority
LEASIB	Local Education Authorities' and Schools' Item Banking Project
MCT	Minimum Competency Testing
NAEP	National Assessment of Educational Progress (US)
NEA	National Education Association (US)
NFER	National Foundation for Educational Research in England and Wales
NUT	National Union of Teachers
OECD	Organisation for Economic Cooperation and Development
PGCE	Post Graduate Certificate of Education
PPBS	Planned Programme Budgeting Systems
PSD	Personal and Social Development (APU)
SAT	Scholastic Aptitude Test (US)
SCISP	Schools Council Integrated Science Project
SCRE	Scottish Council for Research in Education
SSE	School Self Evaluation
SSRC	Social Sciences Research Council
TAMS	Tests of Attainment in Mathematics in Schools (NFER)
VRQ	Verbal Reasoning Quotient

Problem gives rise to problem ...
A strange picture we make on our way to our
Chimaeras, ceaselessly marching, grudging
ourselves the time for rest; indefatigable,
adventurous pioneers.

R L Stevenson, *Virginibus Puerisque*

1 The Urge to Evaluate

Until the early seventies, evaluation was a word rarely heard in schools. Possibly a school might be a test bed for a Schools Council curriculum project, and the word might be used by visiting project staff, applying test instruments to judge its effectiveness with pupils or teachers. Or possibly, as in my own case, one would be in a school committed to curriculum change, and therefore familiar with the litany of aims, learning experiences, selection of content, organisation of learning, evaluation (Wheeler, 1967). This approach had been developed from the American work of Tyler (1949), Bloom (1956) and Taba (1962), using behavioural objectives to postulate curriculum planning as a scientific, feed-forward process. It became known as the objectives model for curriculum development, and its several disadvantages have now become widely recognised (see, for example, Stenhouse, 1975). The model had crossed the Atlantic during the sixties with the establishment of national curriculum development projects by the Nuffield Foundation and the Schools Council, and the research-development-diffusion style adopted by many of these projects was derived from the objectives model. It was based on an implicit analogy between schools and industrial concerns, viewing schools as 'delivery systems'. It plays an important part in the development of formal evaluation strategies.

But at that time, I can remember vividly our own concern with the tasks of design and implementation, as a group of teachers trying to plan a new secondary curriculum. Evaluation was a word which had little to do, it seemed, with the devising of effective classroom experiences. We were not to know, of course, that just as Wheeler's book was published here, one of the American workers in evaluation was publishing a paper which argued strongly against attempts to evaluate effectiveness by measuring performance against behavioural objectives, and proposed instead an approach which judged a school in its context, by the 'countenance' it presented to an observer (Stake, 1967). Certainly, though, the idea that a teacher should consciously adopt ways of evaluating his own performance, or that schools should use devices other than examinations to test pupils' performance, was remote from the work of schools at that time.

What has brought about the extraordinary growth in evaluation studies, and what exactly does it imply? We need first to have a clearer idea of what words like evaluation and assessment actually mean.

Staking Out the Territory

Evaluation is a way of passing judgment on an action. We may watch a carpenter make a joint, and evaluate the action directly; or we may evaluate the competence of a politician by looking at the decisions he took and their effects. In the latter case, though, we need to collect data on his actions and their results, and this will involve some *assessment* of the information that is available, or possibly the generation of new information. How, for example, might we evaluate the performance of Aneurin Bevan in introducing the National Health Service in Great Britain? One would have to determine his intentions and assess their effects. One would certainly be helped by the fact that we can view his actions from the perspective of a quarter of a century. It is easier to disentangle the short-term political arguments and take a more measured view. But the process would, in any event, reflect one's own view of the matter. In selecting which evidence to take and what weight to attach to it, one would be making value judgments which will influence one's interpretation.

It is at once clear that evaluation can be a complex process. But it is also true that, in a more naturalistic sense, it is a process with which we are intensely familiar. When we meet the man who wants to sell us a motor car, we evaluate how he behaves and what he says in deciding how to act. We may, if he looks like ex-President Nixon, decide at once not to buy it from him. And when we decide to switch off a television programme because it is boring, we have made an evaluation of decisions taken by a team of production staff and decided that, by our standards, they are not good enough. We are all, as individuals, privileged to make judgments about other people's decisions, subject to our responsibilities to them and to society.

These responsibilities may not matter much. When I switch off my TV set no one is affected — unless others are watching as well. I may then go and do something else elsewhere, or attempt to make my view prevail. But if I do the latter, I must respect the moral code by which my relations with the others in the room are governed. My evaluation must respond to the *context* of the action, and this may involve social and moral — and political — decisions.

There is another sense, too, in which evaluation is a part of our lives. When we admire the skill of the carpenter, we might aspire to do as well ourselves. Then we must recognise that when the carpenter takes decisions about how he holds his saw, how much pressure he applies and in which direction, he is constantly evaluating what he does and using it to influence the way he continues to do it. He needs to know, of course, much factual information about how sharp his saw is, the nature of the material he is cutting, and the appropriate shape of the joint for the task in hand. But in addition to this *propositional* knowledge — knowing *that* the wood is inclined to split in a certain direction, that four rather than three tongues are needed — he must also possess *procedural* knowledge about *how* he is to go about his task in an effective way. His skill as a craftsman depends on both kinds of knowledge.

Neither is this dependence on both knowing how and knowing that, for satisfactory evaluation and performance, confined to practical activities like woodwork. It is an essential part of the professional equipment of the politician and the teacher. To be successful at the *idiom of the activity* (Oakeshott, 1962), the teacher, like the chess player and the cook, must learn this procedural knowledge by *doing* the activity, and making the process of improving on this doing an implicit part of the activity. Procedural knowledge, in short, rests on an *innate* evaluation of the activity which gives the learner his intuitive professional skill. And while extrinsic evaluation of what he has done will enhance his understanding of his own abilities — if the carpenter's tongues fail to fit the grooves, he is not much good — it is important to recognise that such knowledge cannot by itself lead to improvement: that can only come from successful doing. However rigorously his work is evaluated, the bad carpenter will continue to make ill-fitting joints until his work is informed by this further kind of procedural understanding. The same will be true of the teacher.

Evaluation and Values

I have indicated two ways in which evaluation is ordinarily taken for granted. Innate evaluation as part of an idiomatic activity is of the first importance in any attempt to judge the quality of a professional's work, and I shall return to this in due course. Everyday evaluation of people and events also becomes interesting when it moves outside our privileged personal experience and involves the concerns of others. The example of a number of people watching television, one of whom wishes to extinguish it, is itself trivial but serves to show how easily our own evaluation may affect others. The difficulty of making an evaluation when complex practical actions and the interests of various parties must be considered has long been recognised by establishing legal procedures to decide such actions. In educational evaluation, we ask 'were the right decisions taken?', and to establish this we apply judgment to what we determine as the facts of the case. In law, we ask 'did these events occur?' and reach judgment by a similar two-stage process: we muster and assess the evidence, and make a judgment which evaluates the case.

Note, though, that the early advent of jury systems shows the importance developed societies have attached to devising fair evaluations of what might seem minor events. In the trial by jury of an action for breach of promise, it is a matter of evaluating a series of events in order to establish whether an intention was stated or implied: an intention limited essentially to transactions between two people. Yet it is recognised that each will have his or her own interpretation, to be brought forward as evidence, and that the services of counsel will be needed to present the evidence effectively; and, further, that before an independent group can evaluate the evidence in favour of one or other party, a judge shall assess the evidence and indicate which statements might be of greater consequence than others. It is, in fact, significant that such actions have now become redundant as a result of more informal relationships in society; misunderstandings are less likely to occur. But the point of the example is that, where the rights of individuals are concerned, society does not take up a dismissive line. All legal proceedings are essentially exercises in evaluation, and much weight and ceremony is attached to them. The problematic nature of the exercise is recognised from the start, and elaborate steps are taken to develop adversarial procedures which take account of conflicting interests.

Let us compare such a process with the kind of evaluation which might be carried out by a local authority using its own advisers or inspectors. A senior adviser might form a team from a number of subject advisers, and arrange for individual advisers to observe subject lessons and interview staff over a period of a week or so. At length, a report would be produced for submission to the county education committee as well as the school's governors.

There are grave risks in such a procedure. Because of the various commitments of subject advisers, it is difficult to allocate much time

to the exercise. And while a week might be enough for a team of
HMI to form helpful opinions about a school, HMI have the advantage of both independence and experience. It is clearly impossible for
LEA advisers to close their minds to the various impressions they
have collected about a school, or a particular subject department, in
the course of their regular professional transactions with the school.
Further, advisers have been termed Janus figures: like the Roman
god, they face both ways. Unlike HMI, they are paid by the same authority which runs the school, and have a specific responsibility for
some aspect of the authority's educational programme. They must
offer advice to schools, and yet they must also furnish reports on
schools and their staffs to the authority's officers and elected representatives. There is an ambiguity about their role which can become
disturbing to teachers — and, doubtless, to advisers themselves —
when their brief is not to help the school but to evaluate it. Under
such circumstances, it is not surprising that teachers can feel a particular adviser has misrepresented the true state of affairs, whether or
not any bias was intended. However hard an adviser might try to be
impartial, the basis of the professional activity is fundamentally unsound and both parties are put in a false position.

It is also the case that evaluating educational processes is, like most
arts, one which is improved by practice. The everyday work of subject advisers in listening to a teacher's account of some new curriculum scheme, judging the case put to them for some additional
item of equipment or talking to staff about some educational development thought to be of interest to the school is one thing; making an
assessment of the quality of a teacher's work, the relationships between pupils and the style of discipline and behaviour in a school —
so that a formal evaluation may be presented to those in authority
over the school — is quite another. It is an activity about which many
advisers are uneasy, not least because it can undermine their links
with schools and teachers on which their effectiveness as advisers
must ultimately depend. But it is also an activity with which they are
unfamiliar. HMI, and academics with a professional interest in
evaluation, are experienced teacher-watchers in this sense, and are
also able to judge teachers and schools from a wider perspective than
a particular subject. A collection of reports from a team of subject advisers can scarcely amount to a coherent evaluation of the complex
educational activity of a whole school. These doubts have been put to
me succinctly in a private communication from a head whose school
had been subjected to an adviser-based 'inspection':

I am quite sure that the roles of advisers *qua* advisers and advisers *qua* inspectors are completely irreconcilable. I can see no way in which one can establish an effective, supportive relationship with a teacher, encouraging him in his work, guiding him down fresh paths ... and also write a report which may of necessity be critical of his technique, class control, use of resources and materials or whatever. Apart from anything else, if you have already been working with him *qua* adviser, then any critical comment is implicitly critical of yourself: so how honest can any evaluation be? Furthermore, you may disagree with him fundamentally on a philosophical or conceptual point; but it is the head who determines matters of philosophy, not the adviser or even the CEO. Secondly ... they stand in a much closer, and therefore more vulnerable, relationship to elected members than do teachers in schools. The whole thing is far too parochial.

It is evident that, in the name of evaluation and presumably with the best of intentions, the work of schools, teachers and pupils is likely to be judged in a much more arbitrary way than if an action were being judged in a court of law. And there is the further irony that while a court goes to much trouble to establish judgment where a misdemeanour is concerned, most evaluations of teachers and pupils are evaluations of actions inspired by a professional desire to provide an effective education. They may, indeed, be ineffective actions: but we might suppose that the least we could do, in equity, in making evaluations of such actions is to consider more carefully what is involved before we jump in with both feet.

How Can We Evaluate Education?

On the face of it, it might appear to the man on the Clapham omnibus that evaluating the work of a school is not so very difficult. Surely all we need do is compare examination results? This may seem a naive view, but it is held almost certainly by many who sit on education committees, and who support the publication of league tables of this kind. In parts of the United States, tables comparing the scores of school pupils on achievement tests are shown in estate agents' windows.

One problem is that schools — quite apart from variations in their pupils' social backgrounds — have good and bad years. All teachers are aware of the variation, for no evident reason, between one year's intake and the next. Comparisons are complicated also by the fact that schools use different examinations boards, with different syllabuses and different questions. Also, there is no absolute standard which defines the pass and grade marks each year: the questions obviously have to be different from year to year, and until examiners have seen how candidates answer a question, they cannot tell exactly how difficult it is. Only with very simple mastery skills like typing is it possible to define a grade in absolute terms, by specifying the number of words typed per minute. Current attempts to base a common system of examining at sixteen plus on fixed, invariant criteria fail to take account of the subjective judgments on which standards of performance ultimately rest. Making sensible use of examinations requires much care.

A fundamental difficulty, however, is that if schools are to be judged by examination results, there will be great pressure on schools to reflect this bias in their teaching. And the fact is that although O-level results are generally esteemed by parents and employers, they measure only a small part of what teachers would regard as desirable educational outcomes. They place a premium on propositional knowledge, and on the ability of pupils to recall it. So, evidently, does the public at large, to judge by the popularity of games of the 'mastermind' type. But what is more important is the ability to use this knowledge procedurally, and this calls for more sophisticated types of examination. Although school-based Mode 3 examinations can favour such developments, these have been rarely taken up by schools and are sometimes, quite wrongly, thought to be of lower status than conventional Mode 1 examinations. And by a further irony, examination success in practical subjects like art and design which call for an element of performance is thought to have lower status than in 'academic' subjects like physics and geography.

But even if examinations were set which tested problem solving and creative thinking, there still remains the whole area of a pupil's personal and social development which parents and employers rightly expect a school to foster, but which cannot be tested by standard examinations. So to judge schools solely by conventional examination performance would be tantamount to saying to teachers: 'Don't bother about encouraging pupils to be considerate of others, to learn how to get on with people, to follow through a difficult task with determination and resource, to understand social and political behaviour in our society. Just give them the facts and drills they need to get good grades at O-level and CSE'. If teachers in a school chose to cram cynically for examination success in this way, no doubt they could come out top of the local charts. The price, though, would be paid not only by their own pupils, but also by those in other schools who would appear to be at a disadvantage. It says much for the professionalism of teachers, given the current pressure for examination success, that educational values still hold sway. But as the HMI national secondary survey (DES, 1979) plainly shows, the grip of external examinations has tightened and the effects of this on the curriculum give grave cause for concern.

Over and above all these reasons for seeking to diminish the influence of examinations, there is a further consideration which raises fundamental questions about evaluation.

Measuring Attainment

What examinations, and other tests of attainment or performance, aim to do is allow conclusions to be drawn about educational activities. But there is immediately a conflict between the aim of the educator, which is to help the pupil to achieve understanding, and that of the tester, which is to distill understanding into some observable state. The conflict arises because, as Hirst (1974) points out, there need be no logical connection between a person's state of mind and what we might observe about him or her:

> Achieving understanding does not necessarily result in a person's doing or saying anything of any kind ... And to achieve certain outward and visible signs as the objectives in one's teaching is all too frequently consistent with failing to achieve the state of mind desired ... Most of the central objectives we are interested in in education are not themselves reducible to observable states, and to imagine they are, whatever the basis of that claim, is to lose the heart of the business ... States of mind should never be confused with the evidence for them ... Assessment and evaluation rely on observable evidence, but these evidences are not the object of the teaching enterprise.

When we make comparisons between examination results, whether from school to school or year to year, we are comparing observable evidence but we are certainly not comparing states of educational understanding. Nuttall (1976), writing as secretary of an examinations board, makes the point quite bluntly: 'The message is clear: examination standards do not necessarily tell us anything about educational standards'.

In testing attainment, the tester seeks to establish whether certain educational objectives have been attained, and unless these objectives are clearly formulated from educational criteria, the tests of attainment will fail on educational grounds. 'Tests of rationality are tests to be applied to the *achievements* of one's thought as formulated in propositions, not tests for thought *processes* themselves' (Hirst, op.cit.). Pursuing this argument, McIntyre and Brown (1978) argue that psychometric approaches to the problems of measuring attainment are logically irrelevant: 'It is not how people think or what they do that is being studied, but rather *the evaluations which are made of what they do* ... as soon as criteria of correctness or quality are introduced, one has moved outside a psychological frame of reference.' There are therefore major problems in interpreting scores on attainment tests, and on comparisons between them: and for politicians or administrators to judge school process by the observable evidence of tests is to traduce the educational purpose of schooling. As Soltis (1979) puts it:

> A score of seventy-five per cent on knowledge of rules of the road may be evidence to support a claim of the achievement of the objective of being a safe driver but obviously it is not all that we mean by being a safe driver nor does it even ensure that one will follow the rules of the road once he knows them.

Styles of Evaluation

It should now be clear that evaluation in education is nothing if not a problematic business, and in summarising the nature of the difficulties it is logical to look first at ways in which evaluation might proceed. In considering *how* to evaluate, we can think of a range of approaches with psychometric measurement at one end, and interpretive styles at the other. Lawton (1980) identifies six models:

1 The classical (or agricultural-botanical) research model
2 The research and development (or industrial, factory) model
3 The illuminative (or anthropological, responsive) model
4 The briefing decision-makers (or political) model
5 The teacher as researcher (or professional) model
6 The case-study (or eclectic, portrayal) model

The first two models depend on quantifiable results from tests based on behavioural objectives, and therefore take an impoverished view of educational experience. The third model offers a qualitative account of events: 'Its primary concern is with description and interpretation rather than measurement and prediction' (Parlett and Hamilton, 1972). It aims to offer an 'alternative anthropological paradigm' and in practice draws heavily on observation and interview. But the results of such an evaluation may distort the true values of the events observed just as much as if, using the quantitative approaches of models 1 and 2, one were trying to represent the complex transactions of education as the aggregate of numerical data. It is clear, from the example of a school inspection already given, that an evaluation which does not respond to the intentions of teachers and the learning milieu within which teachers and pupils work will be a partial account in both senses of the word. But we must still decide what meaning to attach to an illuminative evaluation; what weight to give to personal impressions, how far the established procedures of anthropological and historical research can be applied to very recent events and in a quite different context.

The other three models are essentially attempts to meet these objections by leaving room for both quantitative and qualitative techniques to be used within more rigorously defined procedures. Model 4 seeks to make explicit the political stance of the evaluator, and thus clarify one area of interpretive uncertainty. The *bureaucratic* evaluator (MacDonald, 1976) accepts the values of the bureaucrats who hire him, and simply aims to leave behind a satisfied client. Those who devise tests for national and local authorities to implement would evidently come in this category, and we shall see in the next chapter that this style of evaluation prevails widely in the USA. The *autocratic* evaluator sticks to his educational principles, and insists that his advice is taken in devising and interpreting the evaluation. By choosing the right autocratic evaluator to examine a curriculum programme, 'administrators can effectively get what they want without taking the blame for ultimate decisions' (Lawton, 1980). This is also part of the American experience.

The *democratic* evaluator recognises that there is no agreement about fundamental educational issues, and tries to be an 'honest broker', presenting the data without making recommendations. The data are established as a result of 'negotiation' between the evaluator and the evaluated, who retain control of the data and whose contributions stay confidential. This appeals to our sense of fairness, but raises questions about procedure again: can the truth be established by 'negotiating' it? There is, in this context, no absolute truth; by defining the procedure for establishing 'truth' (as in a court of law) we define what we are prepared to accept as 'truth'. The difficulty, again, is that the careers of a number of teachers may depend on what the democratic evaluator presents as truth to the decision-makers.

The *teacher as researcher* model (model 5) shifts the emphasis towards self-evaluation, so that, in Stenhouse's view (1975), the teacher both develops and evaluates the curriculum: 'The curriculum he creates is then to be judged by whether it advances our knowledge rather than by whether it is right. It is conceived as a probe through which to explore and test hypotheses and not as a recommendation to be adopted'. The teacher not only teaches, but assesses what he does in some formal way and seeks to do so objectively. There are parallels with the democratic model of evaluation, and these emerge clearly in the Ford Teaching Project (Elliott and Adelman, 1976) which sought to develop the self-monitoring competence of forty teachers in twelve East Anglian schools. The devices used included field notes made by teachers, tape and tape-slide recordings of lessons, and accounts of lessons offered by independent observers and pupils:

> As participants in the teaching-learning process, pupils are in an extremely good position to provide reliable information about what their teachers do ... A genuine accountability system is something negotiated between the teacher and his audiences. It is a system he freely participates in to support the development of his own self-awareness by checking his tendency to self-deception. (Elliott, 1978)

Using the technique of 'triangulation', the teacher monitors himself by comparing his account of what happened in the classroom with those of pupils and the observer.

This is an elaborate procedure, and in developing formal schemes for individual teachers to monitor themselves in their own classrooms, fails to take account of the invaluable informal ways in which teachers can assess themselves and each other when they work together in planning and implementing new curricula. By focusing on form at the expense of content, it constrains itself needlessly into a rather tortuous view of the business. Stenhouse (1980) remarks that the Ford Teaching Project 'remains an enterprise for enthusiasts, people who tinker in their classrooms as motor-cycle enthusiasts tinker in their back yards'.

Model 6, the case study model, seeks to use eclectically a variety of techniques — measurements, questionnaires, interviews — in examining the entire context of the programme or institution being evaluated. Its advocates see case study not so much as a set procedure but rather an embodiment of particular values and ideas. It deals with real facts, in reporting statements and observations; in portraying the whole scene, it can reveal complexities and conflicts; it can help to establish an archive of interpretable material; and it can offer data in an accessible form.

Case studies can certainly be of great value, and there is considerable American experience to draw upon. But it is plainly an expensive activity, not to be lightly undertaken in any school with a problem; and all the problems of interpretation and objectivity remain. Case study evaluators will have their own political stance, and this may or may not coincide with the stance of those who take decisions on the strength of the study. Despite the emphasis on eclecticism, case study might well become a very personalised affair. Eisner, for example, draws an analogy between appreciating the work of schools and criticism of dramatic performances, and this approach of 'educational connoiseurship' would recognise and value the commitment of the evaluator to particular values, while disclosing 'aspects of the performance that might not otherwise be seen. The critic's language is referentially adequate when its referents can be found in the work or event itself' (Eisner, 1975). Just as Noel Coward's evaluation of a stage production was highly valued, because of his masterly insight into problems of dramatic construction and effect, so some case studies may be esteemed above others not because of their awareness of many points of view and interests, but in spite of them — because the evaluator's own prejudices are seen to be valuable in themselves. The autocratic evaluator might, in fact, be alive and well inside the case study.

This brief look at six methods of evaluating is by no means complete. Stake (1977) lists nine typical evaluation approaches, and it is worth looking quickly at these so as to give another perspective. There are obvious overlaps across the same broad spectrum. *Student gain by testing* uses tests to 'measure student gain in performance', both with and without control groups. *Institutional self-study by staff* involves teachers gathering and interpreting data on their school: 'It is a procedure which honours the *status quo* ... It takes a heavy toll in staff time'. Stake remarks that these two models are very common: 'In any one year at least ten per cent of American teachers and pupils are involved ... in student achievement testing or institutional self-study, as part of a formal evaluation effort'. Next is the *prestige panel* or *blue-ribbon panel*, which has a parallel with the evaluation in the UK of higher education courses by teams from the CNAA[1] (Council for National Academic Awards). The use of similar panels to reinforce in-school evaluations has been advocated in the UK (Becher and Maclure, 1978). *Transaction-observation* is Stake's term for the illuminative model, stressing 'the pluralism of values in education'. *Instructional research* emphasises the experimental nature of any evaluation, seeking to expose new teaching principles and resources under controlled conditions rather than to offer help to the programme's users or sponsors. *Management analysis and social policy analysis* are two similar approaches using concepts drawn from management or the social sciences as analysis tools (cost-benefit analysis, opportunity costs), emphasising efficiency rather than educational values in seeking to define social choices for decision makers (the controversial studies of Coleman and Jencks in the USA of influences on schooling come in this category). *Goal-free evaluation* (Scriven, 1972) distances the evaluator from the intended goals of the programme, so that he attends only to its actual effects. The judgmental role of the evaluator is stressed, and there are perhaps some similarities in style, if not in method, with Eisner's educational connoiseur. Finally, *adversary evaluation* owes much to a legal model, dividing the available resources in two: 'Part to show the shortcomings of the programme, the rest to show merit'.

It may be helpful, too, to add a note on what Stake regards as eight 'common dimensions for classifying evaluation designs'. A pervasive distinction, first made by Scriven (1967) is *formative-summative*: between evaluation during a programme, and evaluation after it is completed. Formative evaluation allows changes to be made; summative evaluation may smack of a summary judgment. In practice, both elements may be present. When a team of advisers 'inspects' a school, the intention is summative but a formative element could arise if there is adequate feedback. The *formal-informal* distinction has already been mentioned: the key point, as Stake recognises, is that formal evaluation is needed 'when the results are to be communicated elsewhere'. A critical distinction is *case particular-generalisation*: is the evaluation simply a study of one programme, or is it a representative study intended to support generalised conclusions? In practice results may lend themselves to generalisation, and the attempt to formulate rules for case study recognises that generalising requires greater control and more regard to setting and context. The *product-process* distinction is a familiar one, and mirrors that between the summative and formative styles of evaluation. The Assessment of Performance Unit (APU) looks only at outcomes, the product of the learning process; yet the HMI national secondary survey (1979) often looks for a contrary emphasis on school practice:

> In many schools, the acquisition of knowledge was the main feature of the science courses; only rarely was the emphasis on teaching the process of science rather than the subject matter.

Harlen (1980) argues that evaluation should reflect this priority: 'If we then take the view that benefit comes from incremental changes, not from general solutions, information about transactions makes possible decisions about changes in transactions which are not possible if one only knows about outcomes'. But who is to measure the transactions, and how?

The *descriptive-judgmental* distinction has already emerged: some compromise must be made between providing information and offering opinion. The *preordinate-responsive* distinction recognises that a preordinate evaluator decides beforehand what he is looking for, while the responsive evaluator is prepared to look at unexpected events which might come to light as he goes along. The *holistic-analytic* boundary separates evaluations which look at the totality of a programme from those which, as in much social-science research, look only at a selection of key characteristics. Case study methods aim for the former. Lastly, the *internal-external* distinction separates evaluations using an institution's own staff from those involving outsiders.

The Scope of Evaluation

After this outline of the complexity with which evaluation issues are clothed, Stake's observation (1977) that 'an evaluation study seems to cost whatever the funding agency can afford' may come as no surprise. Educational evaluation looks for certainties where none exist; so the field is wide open to all comers. Knowing clients will make sure they get the evaluations they want. Banesh Hoffman's pioneering assault on testing (Hoffman, 1962) has gone unheeded; social and political pressures have increased the demand for evaluation exercises, despite their contentious value.

Even the simplest classroom evaluation can be misleading. What should a teacher reward in a piece of writing: good spelling, improvement on other work, the structure, or the total effect? Stibbs (1979) looks at the way a teacher might test a child's reading using a graded word test, and asks:

> What has been tested or measured? It is reading, but reading of single words out of context. The words have no situation which could define their register or meaning ... Is uncontextualised word recognition the sort of reading we really want to assess? ... Even if we are confident that we have correctly judged which words the child has 'read', we cannot be sure that his performance is an accurate reflection of his ability to read in context, and with understanding.

Tests of this kind are said to be criterion-referenced, if they tell us the level of performance achieved by a child rather than how it compares with other pupils. But a norm-referenced reading test makes this comparison, so that a reading age gives the age of pupils who, on average, achieved the same score as the child. Although criterion-referenced tests are often seen as more responsive to the individual conditions of a school and its pupils, the same interpretive difficulties arise. The example of the driving test, given earlier, illustrates this point.

Public examinations, like GCE O-level and CSE, are norm-referenced: there is then, as we have seen, plenty of scope for argument about how the norms are to be defined. The wider we cast the evaluative net, the more we subsume individual uncertainties and errors beneath some overarching measure or generalisation. But the problems of attributing meaning remain: indeed, they are simply magnified as the evaluative scale increases. As House (1973) observes, 'A good motto in evaluation is "think small", both in terms of results and of what it is possible to do'. When a teacher thinks about a child and his work, when he talks to him or watches him in the classroom or laboratory, he makes an assessment which draws on the teacher's educational understanding, his humanity and experience, and his observations of the child over a period of time. It is a transient but defensible judgment; it will be expressed in words and shades of meaning and will not purport to a high measure of accuracy or permanence. A numerical test or an isolated observation misrepresents a complex reality, and the larger the scale of the test the greater the misrepresentation.

It is the case, though, that large-scale evaluations are widely practised, and in separate chapters I shall examine these at three levels. Nationally, the APU testing calls for detailed consideration; locally, the testing programmes of education authorities seem likely to spread; and at school level, there is increasing pressure for formal self-study exercises and reports to be undertaken. There is much to learn from the growth of testing in the USA at all three levels, and this will be discussed in the next chapter. But enough has already been said about the innate difficulty of any form of educational evaluation to lead to the question: who wants to evaluate?

The Climate of Doubt

Evaluation is a form of reassurance. When living standards are rising, economic factors stable or expanding, and when there is optimism about national and world circumstances, the public mood is buoyant and confident and the educational climate is secure and enterprising. But when forebodings arise about trading conditions, when money gets short and insularity prevails, activities like education which depend for their success on trust and optimism are particularly vulnerable to the climate of doubt and fear. Post-war conditions are always favourable to educational reform; hope for a better future reinforces the long-term nature of educational goals and these are carried forward despite adverse economic conditions. By the mid-sixties, this supportive mood had reached its high point. It was unfortunate that it was only at this point that secondary reorganisation took off (and with Crosland's tepid Circular 10 of 1965[2]), and that the Schools Council, which could have done so much for curriculum development, largely dissipated its energies and funds in a welter of projects based on a subject-centred view of curriculum and a bipartite view of schooling.

By the mid-seventies, industrial problems and the 1973 oil crisis had established a quite different climate, and the substantial achievements of comprehensive schools had been set aside in favour of growing criticism of their methods. James Callaghan's speech at Ruskin College[2] caught this mood, and his emphasis on the instrumental aspects of schooling — 'to equip children for a lively, constructive place in society and also to fit them for a job of work' — made a sharp contrast with that on personal development which was eloquently argued in the Plowden Report of 1967. From this point on it was open season for those who were eager to feed doubt with tales of poor school performance. Sections of the press appeared to be in the anxiety industry, seizing on minor incidents in stories which could do considerable harm to the reputation of good schools. And so the 'back to basics' movement broadened its political base, following a pattern which had begun in the USA some five years before.

Three examples will illustrate how insubstantial these criticisms were. First, there was a widespread attack on mixed-ability grouping, along with the suggestion that this was a prominent feature of comprehensive school organisation. The merits or otherwise of this form of grouping are not at issue here: the point is that when HMI published the secondary survey in 1979, it emerged that there was subject setting in two-thirds of the schools, increasing from years 1 to 3, and less than three per cent of the full-range comprehensives surveyed used a full-range mixed-ability organisation in the third year. Stories that comprehensives are monster institutions are in the same category: the average size is about 1000. Second, there were widespread stories of bad behaviour: yet the HMI observed the daily life of 384 schools, and found that 'the very great majority were orderly, hard working, and free from any serious troubles'. Third, much currency was given to the view that comprehensives had perhaps improved standards for average pupils, but only at the expense of the brightest. Although no hard evidence has ever been produced to support this doctrine, some well-known educationists could be heard promulgating it. As a result of a pre-election pledge, the 1979 Thatcher adminstration's assisted places scheme purports to deal with this alleged shortcoming. But in 1980, some findings of the National Children's Bureau longitudinal study of over 6000 pupils at a variety of schools, all born in 1958, show that children of both high and low ability do as well in comprehensives as in selective schools. These results are based on NFER[3]-type attainment tests, and are subject to the reservations one must make about any such tests: but they do at least compare like with like, and this evidence is certainly of a much more substantial calibre than any that has yet been produced to support the opposite suggestion.

It is difficult not to conclude that what matters is not so much the evidence for what is presented as fact, but the context of timing and circumstance. People will believe what they want to hear. And just as in the USA, these misgivings about schooling have led to what has been termed an accountability movement. These issues will be taken further in a later chapter; for the moment, what matters is that an institution can only render an account of its work if an evaluation is carried out. How detailed that evaluation is will depend on the climate of trust and respect which prevails; how reliable that evaluation is will depend, as I have attempted to show, on a great many problematic factors. The feast of accountability celebrates the death of trust: accountability is a social disease, and the cure lies not in schools but in its social origins.

Having said that, there is in fact much to be said for reshaping the secondary curriculum: not because it is too progressive, but because it is too traditional. The case has nothing to do with accountability, but everything to do with a study of education and curriculum. Whole curriculum planning in the secondary school would certainly, on this view, involve a much wider basis for curriculum decision-making than the staff of the school, and would recognise that the views of parents and those who form the school's constituency should be a part of the decision-making process. The result will be greater accountability, but not for its own sake. It will result from professionally-led deliberation about educational effectiveness rather than a philistine rush to measurement and judgment:

> What an evaluation can *never* do is to pronounce authoritatively on future developments, or on what effects the basic idea might have if it were developed in a different way ... Evaluation evidence from a study of work in the field cannot validly be used to discredit the ideas behind the development ... Evaluation will not make our difficult decisions for us; it is a servant, not a master. (Cooper, 1976)

The Limits of Evaluation

Yet there are many influential groups of people who, for one reason or another, are bemused by the false promise of evaluation and would allow it to master educational decision-making. The rites of measurement, the notion that complex human action can be reduced to intervention-counts and test responses, have an appeal for those who put a naive faith in technological rationalism. Schools become little more than factories: delivery systems in which children are the input, teaching the process, and the output is a matter of instructional objectives which can be measured and so used to improve the cycle. (To term this the 'engineering' model, as is often done, is to confuse science with engineering. Engineering, in that it must respond to its context, is at least as much an art as a science.) But the production model seems irresistibly attractive to North Americans:

> Mechanistic analogies have a peculiar appeal for a people who see themselves as the raw materials of a vision which can be socially engineered ... Both the vision and the optimism are reflected in the assumption that goal consensus in education ... is a matter of clarification rather than reconciliation. (MacDonald, 1977)

The production model has clear links with conventional management theory, derived as it is from industrial practice where consensus about profit-centred goals can be taken for granted. Management techniques have been an influential American import into the UK, and it has been fashionable to apply them to the inappropriate sphere of school organisation. Support, therefore, for the doctrine that desired curriculum change will follow objective evaluation of outcomes will be found among heads, teachers and educational administrators as well as those who claim to speak for industry. The justifying concept for this first group of evaluators is *efficiency*.

For a second group, evaluation offers the prospect of *influence* and

administrative tidiness. Systematic evaluation — not necessarily confined to quantitative techniques — will attract those who would reduce school and teacher autonomy in order to promote more cen-
tralist patterns. Thus in Sweden, where central control of education
is well established, public examinations at sixteen have given way to
'a series of standardised tests routinely administered to all children at
certain points in their school careers' (Neave, 1980). The introduction of a similar system in France has not, however, been without
political difficulties. In the UK, the development of the APU as an
arm of the DES (Department of Education and Science) is evidence
that there is support for national monitoring based on achievement
tests. And at local level, the zeal with which politicians and exe-
cutives have embraced testing must raise similar suspicions.

A third group of advocates are drawn to evaluation by expediency.
The idea that a school's work can be boiled down to basic tests and
summary reports has a simplicity which appeals to those for whom
the ambiguities of education seem tiresome or irrelevant. This kind
of reductionism will attract those seeking political *power*, since it is
easily converted to the currency of crude slogans and empty gestures.
It appeals, too, to folk wisdom: the notion that examination results
tell you all you need to know about a school has a homespun simplicity which can easily be evoked on the way to the council chamber or
the ballot box.

Finally, there are those who see educational evaluation as a way of
satisfying professional *curiosity*. Just as scientists seek to know more
and more about less and less, so evaluators hope that a continuing
refinement of analytical instruments will ultimately expose the
mechanism of educational action. One is reminded of the alchemists'
attempts to probe nature's secrets by the pursuit of elaborate rituals.
The search will have a unique appeal for those who would harness
the methods of physical science to an unravelling of educational
issues. With their categories and concepts, these researchers have an
enviable faith in the power of componentisation to reveal complex
truths. And the search may be well rewarded by those who put their
trust in evaluation for more venal reasons. But it may not be entirely
harmless:

> Will our analytic dismantlings of the phenomena of education enable
> us to put together a better, more coherent package, a more worthwhile
> educational experience, or build a better society? Or does the analysis
> do violence to our notion of education? Like others concerned with the
> process of education, the evaluator must choose his methods carefully
> if he is to avoid a charge of vivisection. (Kemmis, 1979)

In any event, the result appears to be an endless eruption of articles and books about assessment, evaluation and accountability, engulfing the real issues of curriculum innovation in an autonomous spiral of academic technology.

It is, of course, the case that under the controlled conditions of scientific experiment, evaluation can throw a sharp light on the theory being tested. And it is an essential part of technological development: whether air deflectors, for instance, on the cabs of lorries reduce air resistance and hence fuel consumption can easily be evaluated outside the laboratory. But once the actions and decisions of people are involved, and political choices are implied, even technology defies straightforward evaluation. It is argued, for example, that the capability of the American Cruise missiles is unproven: the Under-Secretary for Defence 'acknowledges that "it is true we didn't get as many data points as we would like" ', and critics 'have little confidence in test runs on missile ranges in the western United States where the terrain is well known ... Big financial stakes ... will produce a "Cruise missile cartel" unwilling to challenge test results' (*Guardian*, 12 July 1980). Determining the safety of a bridge may seem a much simpler task of evaluation: but test data have to be interpreted by people, and different teams of consutants, asked to state whether the Forth road bridge is safe to all vehicular traffic, have produced sharply conflicting views (*Sunday Times*, 13 April 1980).

However elaborate the technology, analysing the outcomes of human actions depends on contestable human decisions. An ambitious computer traffic forecasting model, costing more than £8m, has produced such unreliable forecasts that the Department of Transport has been advised to abandon it. Instead, the Department 'should be prepared to accept simple methods' (*Guardian*, 25 July 1980).

It might be supposed that when it is a matter of determining the costs of alternative proposals, evaluation becomes simple. On the contrary: the accurate assessment of costs is equally problematic. Urged by the Secretary for the Environment to reduce overspending in local authorities, the Association of Metropolitan Authorities took official data and reached quite different conclusions, depending on how the data were treated. One study showed that Boroughs like Bolton and Leeds were overspending: another the reverse. By the same token, the proposition that the actions of government and civil servants are accountable is a myth, since the evaluation of complex proposals is ultimately a matter of interpretation. The Leitch Report on Trunk Road Assessment, for instance, found no evidence of any link between new roads and economic development.

The fact that no evidence exists — that no satisfactory evaluation can be made — is not, however, an argument for rejecting a proposed course of action. It suggests rather that the focus should move to the reasons for the proposal, and the way in which the decision has been reached. If we allow ourselves to believe that a decision can be justified in terms of its effects, however assessed, we may well be inclined to give insufficient attention to the process of discussion and deliberation which originally gave rise to the decision.

The effects of educational decisions are at least as difficult to assess as the social and economic decisions mentioned above (and which have been reported over a very brief period of time). Similarly, the arguments for or against any educational decision always involve conflicting values: indeed, the solution of curriculum problems can brutally expose inadequacies in the reasoning process. (It is said that the office of Education Secretary is regarded as a politician's graveyard: it certainly has a cruel way of exposing reputations.)

Education, then, is *par excellence* a field in which everything depends on value judgments. There is no value-free evaluation, no easy way of judging curriculum activity. Yet the belief persists that formal evaluation can and must be done. I have argued that it cannot be done in an unambiguous way, and furthermore that there are reasons why it often should not be done. In the following chapters I shall look closely at a number of current attempts to apply evaluation techniques to schools, and conclude with some suggestions for shifting the emphasis quite radically: away from misleading attempts to evaluate decisions, and towards better ways of making decisions. Concentrating on the input to the curriculum process rather than the output offers none of the easy answers so eagerly sought after by the evaluating legions: but it does put value judgment squarely in the centre of the argument. The real danger of evaluation is that the 'big science' of evaluative technique will push value issues aside. In a high technology society, it is too easy to be mesmerised by functional analysis and forget that education depends on human perception and understanding.

NOTES

1 **CNAA.** The Council for National Academic Awards is an autonomous body set up in 1964 to award degrees to students in educational institutions, such as colleges of higher education and polytechnics. Pro-

posals for such courses are devised by the institutions themselves and submitted to the CNAA for approval. The CNAA appoints a validating team who meet the staff responsible for the proposal, frequently visiting the institution to inspect facilities and make an on-the-spot evaluation of the scheme.

2 **Crosland and Callaghan.** Anthony Crosland was Minister of Education from 1965 to 1967, during the 1964-70 Labour administration with Harold Wilson as Prime Minister. In 1965 he took the decision to publish DES Circular 10, which requested local education authorities to submit plans for the reorganisation of secondary education into a system of comprehensive schools. The Circular allowed a great variety of plans to proliferate, with many different ages of transfer between schools; it also failed to give any lead regarding the educational tasks appropriate to a comprehensive school. It has been argued that a more forceful circular at this time might have speeded reorganisation and eliminated much of the subsequent bickering.

By 1976, James Callaghan had been leading a Labour administration for two years. Again, it could be argued that his Ruskin College speech was necessitated by the failure of the 1964 administration to clear up uncertainties about what the comprehensive school was in business to do.

3 **NFER.** The National Foundation for Educational Research in England and Wales is an independent organisation 'devoted to progress in education'. It is financed mainly by the local education authorities and the Department of Education and Science, and also receives support from teachers' organisations and universities. It undertakes and publishes research, and has a long-standing interest in the construction of tests.

In common usage the term NFER has been applied interchangeably to both the National Foundation for Educational Research in England and Wales (an advisory and research-oriented body enjoying charitable status) and the NFER Publishing Company, a limited company 'engaged in the publishing of original research and research related material from all parts of the educational field as well as from the Foundation itself' and run as a commercial enterprise.

In general, reference in this book to 'the NFER' should be taken to mean 'the Research Foundation'. The above note, however, will have indicated that it is not always convenient or possible to distinguish the Research Foundation from the Publishing Company. In the following text, where the Publishing Company is explicitly meant in a reference to 'the NFER', it will be marked by a dagger, thus: NFER[†]. The reference in this chapter (p. 28) to 'NFER-type attainment tests' is to tests devised by the Research Foundation and published by the Publishing Company.

In 1981, while this book was 'in press', it was formally announced that the NFER Publishing Company had entered into a partnership arrangement with the commercial publishers Thomas Nelson and Sons Ltd and that the partnership company would trade under the name NFER-Nelson Publishing Company Ltd.

2 Evaluation: An American Dream

The study of curriculum design, implementation, change and evaluation first became a major field of intellectual activity in the USA. This was largely the result of the American need to tackle, as a cultural imperative, the task of mass general education. In England, we have only come to take note of pioneering American work in curriculum studies as we have moved, cautiously but ineluctably, from a divided view of education to one which recognises the need to offer all children meaningful cultural experiences. English education owes much to its nineteenth-century origins, and to the distinction between an elite education for future leaders and a basic education for those born to follow. National responsibility for secondary education for all was not accepted until the 1944 Education Act, and the concept only took shape in an institutional format as comprehensive schools were formed in the 1960s. By this time national curriculum development projects were well established in the USA, and in due course these became a part of the British educational scene. The emphasis in both countries was, however, on updating subject content rather than re-thinking the shape of the whole curriculum to meet the new demands being made on it. In the USA, new thinking was constrained by an emphasis on technocratic models of curriculum process: in the UK, by the ubiquitous grammar-school model of secondary education. British shortcomings became evident during the early seventies, as the first cohort of pupils to receive five years' compulsory secondary education came through the system, emerging in the summer of 1974. Finally, in 1977, with the publication of the Green Paper *Education in Schools: A Consultative Document* by the Callaghan administration, the connection was made at official level between compulsory secondary education for all and the tasks of whole curriculum planning.

American concern to establish an equitable system of public education doubtless assisted the remarkable expansion of the American economy during the first half of this century. Certainly, though, this expansion was the result of an emphasis on free competition and the ethics and rewards of the market place. The results of scientific research were used to update commercial products, and skilfully sold to a public encouraged to put a premium on novelty. Technology — as systematic, science-inspired thinking — could both manufacture and manipulate. Given clear ends and sufficient means, it could put a man on the moon *and* solve the problems of the human psyche.

These values were reflected in American education. The emphasis on improvement, on science-based methods and on the ultimate solubility of every problem gave a distinctive behaviourist[1] slant to American psychology and wide currency to testing as a measure of pupil response. And when eventually, in the late sixties, the fruits of this faith began to turn sour, it was inevitable that Americans would rely on the same technocratic devices to put matters right. After the usual transatlantic time-lag our own society developed the same economic sickness, and turned to American remedies. Some regard for the evaluation scene in the USA is therefore a necessary stage in understanding what has happened here, and what might happen next. As MacDonald remarks (1976), 'We in Britain are fledgelings in a specialism that is well established across the Atlantic'.

Testing as a Way of Life

The influence of the stimulus-response approach of the psychologist Skinner on American education cannot be under-estimated. It argues that a complex activity, like learning, can be reduced to manipulable scale simply by codifying the outputs to known inputs and without requiring any understanding of the intervening process. Thus mind becomes a mechanism, and yields to the whole apparatus of science; of graphs, diagrams, statistical analysis and the blueprint for next year's model. The same means-end analogy can be transferred to business, commerce and the design of educational programmes: simply define the objectives in terms compatible with the available technology, and these will in turn define the appropriate means and furnish a method by which success or failure can be established. A speaker at an American conference on 'Applied Performance Testing' (Lavisky, 1975), reveals clearly how far behaviourism is virtually a cultural artefact:

> Accountability is a goal-directed management process. So it is easy to see how it ties into the behavioural-objectives movement ... Here we have the confluence of one movement which says that school ad-

ministrators have to specify their purposes and accomplishments in a way that is susceptible to assessment, and another movement that says 'here is the way you can specify instructional objectives to make them measurable.' Don't they fit together nicely? ... To move toward the education end will take time, effort, imagination and ingenuity ... We're in good company because the instructional technologists and the systems analysts are all wrestling with the same problem. If, and when, we and they develop tools and techniques for reducing our global educational goals to discrete, behavioural objectives, the rest of the job will be much, much easier.

American teachers seem generally to share this faith in the power of scientific ratiocination to illuminate their work, and have always tended to use tests as diagnostic instruments to a much greater extent than in Britain. But the step from achievement testing to accountability took a little time, and had its beginnings in the post-war enthusiasm for up-dating mathematics and science teaching in American schools. Academic figures had developed war-winning weapons; who better to develop curriculum projects which would match school learning to new discoveries? The Russian Sputnik went into orbit as the first projects were under way, and within a year Congress had passed the National Defense Education Act of 1958. Federal funding of school programmes was generally welcomed, despite the long-standing tradition of local and professional autonomy. The long-term implications were unforeseen.

Introduction of these projects to schools during the 1960s followed the research-development-diffusion style: the assumption was that the results of expert research would be developed in trial schools, and take-up would follow just as a new industrial product is test-marketed and then sold. A new optimism enabled Lyndon Johnson to establish a compensatory education programme, and national intervention increased. But by the late sixties, the economy had declined and the Vietnam war led to a mood of self-criticism. As national consensus waned, special interest groups representing the able, the disabled, women and ethnic minorities became more prominent. Atkin (1980) has argued that as a result of this process a federal law, 'intended by the Congress to assure that the rights of the handicapped are protected, represents one of the sharpest intrusions of the federal government into the details of teaching practice'.

By the early seventies, test results were being used as evidence of decline in school standards. The Scholastic Aptitude Test (SAT) was a convenient yardstick, since the USA has no system of public examinations like GCE and CSE, and no advisers or inspectors. The

SAT is a qualification for university entrance, and widely used as the sole criterion: 'People are moving toward making decisions on the basis of the tests because it is easy and gives it a kind of scientific validity' (the director of admissions at Harvard, quoted in *The Times Higher Education Supplement*, 18 July 1980). Yet an earlier Harvard report (*THES*, 25 January 1980) concluded that, contrary to the claims of the Education Testing Service which devises the SAT, 'the test adds little to the predictive value of high school grades' and 'students' scores on the tests can be improved with coaching'. The fact, therefore, that between 1967 and 1977 the SAT showed declines of eight per cent on verbal and five per cent on mathematical skills needs careful interpretation.

Eventually, in 1977, the US Department of Health, Education and Welfare (HEW) established a 'task force' of administrators and academics to pronounce on 'the national concern with basic skills and minimum competency'. It concluded that the decline in test scores had four within-school causes. First, 'the past twenty years have seen a proliferation of subject-matter courses available to pupils', many as a result of 'external pressures'. Pupils were free to choose less rigorous courses. Second, teachers were confused about their roles: they had been given 'new and often contradictory models of appropriate pedagogic behaviour'. Third, less pupil time was spent 'on task': 'an extraordinary amount of school time is spent on transitions from class to class, routines, announcements ... control and discipline'. And last, there were fewer opportunities 'for intensive study in selective academic environments'. But there were reservations about the value of tests: 'for diagnostic purposes, again the item selection techniques of our main standardised tests make them unsuitable for diagnosis ... Giving one big test is not a very efficient way'. Furthermore,

> Setting minimum competency standards ... is the final step in a completely unsuccessful effort to reduce to precise behavioural terms what education is all about. Attempts to impose competency-based teacher education ... have surely failed ... Knowledge and skill cannot be divided into hundreds of discrete objectives. (National Academy of Education, 1979)

National Testing Takes Off

By this time, however, it was too late to make reservations. The USA had seized the notion of educational accountability with both hands. The initiating agency for this policy was the National Assessment of Educational Progress (NAEP)[2], a body first set up in 1967. NAEP was the precursor of the British APU, and was run by an interstate commission roughly equivalent to the NFER in the UK. The purpose of NAEP was to obtain hard data about school performance for use in federal policy decisions. (This attachment to 'macro indicators' and manpower planning in the Kennedy-MacNamara years was reflected in the UK in Harold Wilson's 'white heat of technology' campaign of 1964.) The NAEP proposal to survey educational outcomes nationally had at first met with resistance from local administrators and union leaders, fearing invidious comparisons between schools, a backwash effect on the curriculum and federal intrusion into local affairs. But with heavy federal funding of curriculum projects, the piper was beginning to call the tune; and already a consequence of this funding was the widespread evaluation of projects by funding agencies. In the event, the opponents of NAEP were bought off by the classic device of putting them on the organising committee. When a DES-sponsored team visited the USA in 1976 to examine testing programmes, they remarked that 'One might observe cynically ... that opposition at that point largely died away, despite there being no discernible change in policy' (Burstall and Kay, 1978). By then, the DES had used the same dodge in setting up its own equivalent of NAEP, the APU.

The original NAEP surveys were guided by a list of fifteen objectives, the first of which was 'To obtain meaningful national data on the strengths and weaknesses of American education (by locating deficiencies and inequalities, in particular subject areas and particular subgroups of the population)'. This was dropped in 1974, when the NAEP aims were recast into eight 'goals'. There is, as we shall see, another interesting parallel here with the evolution of the APU. For the moment, listing goals 1, 4, 6, 7 and 8 will convey the flavour of the operation:

To measure change in the educational attainments of young Americans

To provide data, analyses and reports understandable to, interpretable by, and responsive to, the needs of a variety of audiences

To facilitate the use of NAEP technology at state and local levels when appropriate

To continue to develop, test and refine the technologies necessary for gathering and analysing NAEP achievement data

To conduct an ongoing programme of research and operational

studies necessary for the resolution of problems and refinement of the NAEP mode.

It is convenient at this point to set out the APU's official terms of reference, re-arranging their order so as to allow direct comparison to be made:

To promote the development of methods of assessing and monitoring the achievement of children at school, and to seek to identify the incidence of under-achievement

To identify significant differences of achievement related to the circumstances in which children learn, including the incidence of under-achievement, and to make the findings available to those concerned with resource allocation within government departments, local education authorities and schools

To promote the conduct of assessment in cooperation with local education authorities and teachers

To identify and appraise existing instruments and methods of assessment which may be relevant for these purposes

To sponsor the creation of new instruments and techniques for assessment, having due regard to statistical and sampling methods.

The similarities are quite striking, and so is the much more direct and explicit language used in the American original.

From the beginning, NAEP administered its tests by matrix sampling, with no more than twelve pupils tested in any one school, and the schools picked so as to form a representative set. Testing is at four ages: 9, 13, 17 and 'young adults' of 26-35. (APU testing is at ages 11, 13 and 15.) NAEP evaluates performance in ten curricular areas, which mainly reflect school subjects: mathematics, science, reading, writing, literature, citizenship, career and occupational development, social studies, music and art. What were termed 'intangibles' — attitudes, habits and values — aroused concern at first on the organising committee, but have now been built into tests in each subject area. No individual child, teacher or school can be identified. There were, however, no difficulties in gathering background information about pupils and teachers at the time of testing, including details of home life and attitudes, and pupils' opinions of their teachers' methods. American objections did not at first focus on the process of testing, which was assumed to be a virtuous activity in its own right: the argument was about the use to which test data might be put.

A NAEP exercise is timed to take thirty-five minutes, plus fifteen minutes to administer it. Many of the exercises, according to another DES-sponsored team which visited the USA in 1978, 'follow the familiar machine-stored multiple-choice format in which the respondent darkens an oval on his answer sheet to indicate his answer' (Black and Marjoram, 1979). Only two or three of the ten areas are tested each year, perhaps together with a 'special probe' testing of 'basic life skills' or 'consumerism'. It takes six years for the assessment of a single area to work through the development-administration-analysis-reporting cycle. Areas are re-assessed at two to six year intervals. The results aim to show how well the nation, and groups within it, meet specified goals. Group results are given by sex, race, geographic region, parental education, community size and type, as well as age. The underlying concept is that of mastery learning: has this group mastered this knowledge? The test contractors tailor their wares to fit three key guidelines, defined by NAEP. First, there must be *content validity*: the test is supposed to measure the knowledge, attitude or skill defined by the objective. These judgments are made by psychometricians and subject matter specialists. Second, the *difficulty level* must be specified: the aim is to describe the performance of the most able, least able and average students. Trial exercises must be tested in the field. Third, the *format* of the exercise ought to be that most appropriate for a given objective, but anything other than a paper-and-pencil test is much more expensive to carry out. Financial pressure favours machine-marked multiple choice tests, and NAEP is short of funds. NAEP describes its exercises as 'objectives-referenced', which would make them more criterion than norm-referenced. The fact is that the line between these two styles, however, is not easily drawn. Although NAEP publications often contrast their tests with norm-referenced tests, Greenbaum *et al.* (1977) concluded that the NAEP tests 'are not in any meaningful sense criterion-referenced'. Burstall and Kay (1978) give some examples of NAEP reading exercises.Here is one of them:

Read the story about a fish and answer the question which follows it.

Once there was a fish named Big Eyes who was tired of swimming. He wanted to get out of the water and walk like other animals do. So one day without telling anyone, he just jumped out of the water, put on his shoes and took a long walk around the park.

What did the person who wrote this story want you to do when you read it?   Cry
                   Yell
                   Laugh
                   Become angry
                   I don't know.

It is not easy to determine what benefits have accrued from all this effort. Black and Marjoram (1979) found that in Washington, government officials 'admitted that the findings had only a partial effect on policy and did not seem to expect otherwise'. The secretary of the National Science Teachers Association 'felt that on the whole teachers had not learnt very much from the actual tests set by national assessment'. In a detailed report on the NAEP science assessments, such results emerge as: boys did better than girls; variation was as expected between parental education, and whites and blacks; 'almost all Americans have some idea of what the scientific method is ... '; 'a majority of young Americans approve the idea of research in pollution, population control and atomic energy'.

In 1979, the federal grip on NAEP tightened when it was decided that the NAEP operation must be put out to open tender. Although the ECS is expected to be chosen in view of its past experience with NAEP, future assessment contracts will be supervised by a policy committee representing industry and the public as well as teachers and legislators, and responsible for defining goals and learning areas. In 1979 the DES sent a third team to look at the American testing scene, and they reported (Pring and Selby, 1980) that NAEP and ECS officials, in reviewing this reorganisation, consider it 'cannot be dissociated from the more general move in the 1970s to make schools more accountable to central government especially in the so-called basic skills ... NAEP was clearly a likely instrument for conducting such testing ... ' The move was resisted 'by those who shared its original aims and philosophy'.

Testing at Local Level

A number of states already had testing programmes established by the late sixties. By 1975 most had programmes of some kind or other under way, and between 1975 and 1978 state officials and legislators rushed to introduce basic skills testing as the 'back to basics' movement peaked. By 1980 it was reported (*The Times Educational Supplement*, 15 February 1980) that of the fifty states, thirty-seven had introduced minimum competency testing (MCT) in some form. It looked, however, as if few of the remaining thirteen states would now follow suit: the rush to test had at last slowed down. In nineteen states, MCT is linked to high school graduation at grade nine (age fourteen-plus): to get a leaving diploma, pupils must show a minimum competence at basic skills, usually reading, writing and mathematics. In the other eighteen states, MCT is justified as a screening device to identify pupils who need remedial help.

The growth of statewide testing during the seventies can be followed by examining the reports of the three DES missions. In each case, an HMI directly involved with the APU was accompanied by an academic, whose specialism reflected the purpose of the visit. On the first mission, the HMI then in charge of the APU (Brian Kay) went with the Deputy Director of the NFER (Clare Burstall): the emphasis was on methods of assessment and the technical problems of testing. The NFER is the major contractor for the APU operation and the issues of administering, reporting and interpreting dominate the report. Two years later, in 1978, the next head of the APU (Tom Marjoram HMI) was accompanied by Professor Paul Black, Director of the Centre for Science Education at Chelsea College, University of London, and which, with the University of Leeds, had been awarded the contract to construct and administer the APU science tests ready for use from 1980. They found that much had changed, and recommended further annual visits. In 1979 the focus of interest was the work of the APU exploratory group in personal and social development, and an HMI in the APU (Colin Selby) was accompanied by Professor Richard Pring of Exeter University, a philosopher of education and a member of the exploratory group. While the three reports obviously reflect their different purposes and authors, my impression is that they disclose an increasingly critical view of the American testing scene as the decade wore on. The discussion of the state testing scene shows this to some extent.

The Burstall/Kay report looked closely at practice and intentions in Oregon, Michigan, Georgia and California. The Black/Marjoram report describes the Florida scheme in detail, and outlines the schemes in New Jersey, Georgia and Massachusetts. The Pring/Selby report looks at recent developments in California, Florida, Illinois, Michigan and the City of Chicago. Differences in the schemes arise from differences in state politics and administration, and different traditions of school board autonomy within a state. None is representative, but the California scheme is worth outlining, if only because, as Atkin (1980) remarks, 'California often acts first and most thoughtlessly in the US, but it often offers precursors of programmes that will surface in similar form elsewhere'.

The California state testing programme began in 1961. Results are compared between school districts, and analysed to show the effect of achievement in the previous grade, the proportion of 'limited or non-English speaking' pupils in the schools, and the percentage receiving

'Aid to Families with Dependent Children'. Children are tested at age seven, eight, eleven and seventeen in reading, written expression, spelling and mathematics. The tests are applied by matrix sampling and then presented at school, district and state levels. Burstall and Kay (1978) reproduce the computer print-out report for the second and third grade (age seven and eight) reading tests in spring 1974 for the Keenan School in the Bassett Unified District of Los Angeles County. The mean test score for second-graders in the school is 51.9, compared with 58.5 in the district, 66.6 in the state and 63.9 for the entire nation. One is also told that 'For grade two your school's score is below the comparison score range for schools like yours', and that 'Your school's socioeconomic indication is higher than thirty per cent of all other schools'. Scores are given for no less that fourteen separate 'content areas': *word identification,* sight words, phonetic analysis, consonants, vowels, *vocabulary,* denotation, relational, synonyms, *comprehension,* literal, details, interpretive, and *study-locational* (the four main areas are in italics). Percentile ranks for each are shown as positions and standard error range on the 'state percentile rank scale', in order to 'discourage over-interpretation of small differences in subtest scores'. If the bands do not overlap, this may indicate 'more important differences ... For example, bands do not overlap for consonants and vowels. The importance of this difference can only be determined in the context of your instructional program'.

The Burstall/Kay report remarked that state assessment procedures 'might be highly relevant to the application by LEAs for their own monitoring exercises of assessment techniques developed through the APU or on similar lines'. They compare the California scheme favourably with that in Michigan, where 'schools of widely different opportunities are being publicly subjected to comparison on these inadequate criteria'. They considered that the California programme 'to some extent escapes those criticisms ... no information can be derived about individual classes or individual pupils'. Two years later, Pring and Selby (1980), noting that during their visit to the state education department 'a mother came for the computer print-outs to help her decide where to buy a house', list three criticisms of the California assessment tests:

> The first is that the objective type tests assess only certain kinds of learning. The second is that the few background variables chosen do not explain (away) sufficiently some of the differences in achievement, and that the results imply school responsibility for results that are due to influences beyond their control. Thirdly, ... teachers felt forced to teach to the tests to the neglect of other areas of the curriculum in-

cluding science or indeed of the more educative aspects of the areas being tested.

In addition to all this, however, California administers two other test programmes. One is a set of norm-referenced tests of three federally-funded programmes (for compensatory education, disadvantaged youth and bilingual pupils). The other is minimum competency testing at grades six, nine and eleven (ages eleven, fourteen and sixteen), and each school district sets its own MCT tests. From 1980, award of a high school diploma will be tied to MCT performance. But in Florida, a federal court has ruled that such a step must be postponed for four years, on the grounds that the test was unfair to black candidates who may spend their first three years of education in inferior segregated schools. In 1979 blacks represented nineteen per cent of Florida school leavers, and sixty-four per cent of pupils failing the test three times were blacks. MCT was adopted by Florida in 1976, a main aim being 'to provide information about costs of educational programmes and the differential effectiveness of different instructional programmes'. But then, as House (1973) had pointed out, 'Whatever else accountability may be, it is a way of holding down spending'. Economic factors obliged Florida to eliminate science from its MCT programme. The 'standards' in reading, writing and mathematics are published, and Black and Marjoram (1979) give as an example one of the reading standards: 'The student will recognise fantasy, fact and opinion in a message'. Evidence that the MCT programme has a backwash effect on the curriculum comes from the results of a questionnaire, which showed that about half of a sample of 1200 teachers 'used the results to design changes in their curricula'. Black and Marjoram comment that 'The narrowing effect of the limited range of subjects tested and of the limited test techniques ... does not seem to be a cause for concern'. They note that 'the minimum competency philosophy tends to produce narrowed focus on basic skills and may paradoxically actually result in a lowering of standards ... the responses evoked by standardised testing may bear little relationship either to the abilities that most pupils possess or to the skills and attitudes that teachers are trying to instill'.

The use of MCT was pioneered by Michigan, where an undertaking not to release individual school results had been given by the state education authority. Political pressure forced the state to renege on this, and this provoked the first serious criticism of testing from American teachers. There was further concern in 1971, when a compensatory education programme was tied to the MCT results. This would have identified low-achievers using locally defined standards, and continued to provide extra funds only to those schools showing satisfactory improvement in pupil scores. A major outcry obliged the state to back down, and not withhold funds from low-scoring districts.

Michigan teachers, however, have had to learn to live with MCT league tables, and the administrators in the state have attached much importance to the public presentation of results. Pring and Selby (1980) quote at length from guidance documents issued by the state department of education:

> The Parent Pamphlet, in conjunction with the Item and Objective Handbook and teacher explanations, will help to create the home-school partnership for building better basics ... Your assessment results have the potential for an excellent public relations opportunity ... If possible, meet with media representatives to discuss the release ... and clarify what the schools are trying to do ... Be positive and honest in presenting results. Even if the results are less than 'glowing', acknowledge needs openly ... Do not attach blame to socioeconometric status for low test results. Finally, request the film *Building Better Basics: the Home-School Partnership* ... It should be useful in any parent-teacher meeting ...

The Reaction Against Testing

The application of performance tests to determine pupil learnings can be criticised on three counts. First, and fundamentally, the *meaning* of the tests can be called to account, by asking: What is the connection between the results and the educational process they purport to measure? Academics may question the technicalities of the way a test is constructed, in a number of ways, and to testing technologists some tests may be arguably better — more competently executed — than others. At a deeper level, there are philosophical issues concerning the nature of knowledge and the evidence for its acquisition. These criticisms have been put in plain language by the American John Holt (1970):

> I do not think that testing is necessary, or useful, or even excusable. At best, testing does more harm than good; at worst, it hinders, distorts, and corrupts the learning process ... Our chief concern should not be to improve testing, but to find ways to eliminate it ... How can we expect to measure the contents of someone else's mind when it is so difficult, so nearly impossible, to know more than a very small part of the contents of our own?

But the prevailing attitude of American teachers is quite different. On their 1976 visit, Burstall and Kay (1978) found that 'Many of them are very much aware of the "objectives" of their teaching programme and consciously teach to them so that they are sympathetic to the whole process of defining outcomes and testing them'.

It is, though, possible to support the general idea of testing but object to the *scale* with which it is implemented. This second line of criticism asks: when does the scale of testing threaten teacher and pupil? What outcomes are suitable for testing, and to what extent? A teacher, for example, may apply a diagnostic test to all the pupils in his class, to establish which need extra help. But if the school applies the same test to all the pupils in that year, comparisons may be made between teacher and pupil performance on inadequate evidence. Burstall and Kay criticise the Michigan testing scheme on these grounds:

> The Michigan experience provides not only a vivid demonstration of the ways in which the every pupil model of testing can lend itself to the misuse of test data, but also gives some indication of the wastefulness of the model in terms of the financial outlay involved and the administrative burden imposed on the school system, to say nothing of the sheer weight of testing borne by the individual pupil.

For them, it was the scale, not the nature of testing, that was wrong: matrix sampling would put matters right.

A third line of criticism still remains, however: To what *use* will the results of testing, however carried out, be put? Plainly, the bigger the scale of the test, and the more ambitious its intentions, the greater the interest in using the results. And on each of the three grounds for criticising testing, one can ask: what are the effects — whether direct or indirect — on the teacher, and on the pupil?

The NAEP scheme has the benefit of substantial academic support in developing its tests, and matrix sampling side-steps some of the criticisms of scale. But it must still be shown to be beneficial and not harmful, and a major issue is the way in which the results are presented. This was of particular interest to Burstall and Kay, because of the similarities between NAEP and the APU, and the hope of learning from the NAEP experience. They found that 'The extent to which NAEP should limit itself to providing information and leave it to others to interpret its findings seems to have been a matter of debate from the beginning'. The basic problem is that the more interpretation is offered, the more influential the results — and hence the greater the backwash effect on the curriculum. To the hardliner politicians, the backwash can only be good news — teachers will teach what really matters. But to educationists, interpretation raises a host of doubts about the connection between testing, teaching and learning. In any event, Burstall and Kay found that HEW officials in Washington 'said that national assessment data had not been used to set priorities or stimulate either legislative or programme changes ... NAEP has had virtually no influence on policy decisions'.

Two years later, as has been noted, Black and Marjoram (1979) confirmed that NAEP results had only partially affected policy. The officials, however, went on to tell them that 'one of the great assets of national assessment has been the way in which it has helped individual states to get on with their programmes'. Some states had adopted 'miniature replications' of NAEP procedures, twenty others were using NAEP items, and four more used NAEP technical advice. Inasmuch as NAEP represents a level of testing competence, academics might welcome this wider influence: it has been argued that the NAEP item banks, containing the exercises and information on content validity and difficulty levels, should be entirely open. But how much influence is desirable? What happens when states use NAEP tests on a blanket basis, as in Michigan? And what happens when blanket testing turns into minimum competency testing of only English and mathematics, as in Florida?

In any case, it is scarcely possible to make a national testing operation like NAEP totally secret: apart from the political difficulties, the academic community cannot be sworn to silence, and testing needs its help. Inevitably, national testing cannot be separated from local testing. And the virtues of national testing can become vices when applied locally: yet control of local testing by the federal authority places quite unacceptable constraints on local autonomy. The problem with testing is not knowing how to start, but knowing when to stop.

The problem has been squarely and impressively faced by the National Education Association (NEA), which is by far the largest teachers' union in the USA. In a monograph *Alternatives to Standardised Testing* (1977), published after an NEA 'task force' had concluded that 'the intended purposes of testing can be accomplished ... through a variety of alternatives to tests', the NEA declared that 'The use of evaluation for categorising and tracking students and for denying them educational opportunities should be de-emphasised in favour of constructive, diagnostic, helping purposes'. While supporting 'Frequent and comprehensive evaluation of student learning progress', and the use of 'carefully developed criterion-referenced tests, and teacher-made tests', the NEA opposes 'Reliance on any single system, process, or instrument for making decisions about students' learning potential and progress', and 'The use of tests for determining the allocation of school funds'. This document leaves room for some kinds of testing, but is none the less a major assault on traditional teacher testing wisdom, and the academic testing establishment, in the USA:

> Standardised tests measure cognitive learnings almost totally, thus their content leaves vast and important affective and psychomotor learning areas almost completely untouched ... Consequently, large and important segments of education in the social and behavioural sciences, the arts, even the physical sciences are likely to be given short shrift ... Then there is the heavy emphasis on multiple-choice items ... Students who think most penetratingly and creatively can frequently justify more than one plausible answer for these ... Finally, standardised achievement, aptitude, and intelligence tests are culturally biased ... There may be a lot right about middle-class culture and values, but in a pluralistic society the question needs to be raised: How much of such culture and how many of such values are appropriate to all segments of society and thus should be reflected in educational measurement and evaluation? (Quinto and McKenna, 1977)

They list five alternatives to testing: contracts with students (where the teacher agrees defined outputs with the student), the interview (evaluation by 'direct oral communication with students'), teacher-made tests, criterion-referenced tests, and open admission (admitting students to all programmes, using 'no tests at all').

An important NEA initiative was to fund and publish a report (Tyler *et al.*, 1978) by a 'blue-ribbon' panel of independent educationists into the Florida accountability programme. It concluded that:

> The strategy adopted in the statewide MCT programme ... is seriously faulty ... A strategy likely to be more effective in improving education in Florida would have helped schools to identify their particular problems ... The panel also finds the implementation faulty ... due largely to excessive haste in instituting the programme and failure to ... involve all those who are responsible for making the programme work and those who are seriously affected by it.

The panel recommended that the state department of education 'shift its emphasis more sharply from acting to regulate, control, and direct education in the state to *furnishing leadership in the clarification of critical educational issues* and *providing technical assistance to local schools* ... ' (italics in the original). The NEA had taken a similar step in 1972, when it financed an independent study of the Michigan accountability scheme (House, Rivers and Stuffelbeam, 1974). The study concluded that 'Test results are not good measures of what is taught in school', and 'unless one teaches the tests themselves, they are not very sensitive to school learning'. The practice of tying test results to school funding was condemned as 'whimsical' and 'harmful'.

In 1978, the NEA published a booklet *Back to the Basics?* (Snider, 1978) which put the argument about testing and accountability in its educational context. This 'position paper' was prepared by the NEA's 'instruction and professional development staff', and comments were invited. Initiatives of this kind and quality do not often appear from teachers' organisations in the UK. It asks, what are the basics? According to an open letter to President Carter from three hundred teachers, 'What is basic in education is meeting the need for all pupils in society to learn to the fullest extent of their needs, desires, and capabilities'. Basics involve the whole nature of education, and 'hard thinking about the more basic policy questions' is needed. Reviewing the post-war background, the sixties are seen as

> a crazy quilt of new programs as the US Office of Education became a bureaucratic conduit for federal funds to support such diverse innovations as new math, language laboratories, teaching machines, and instructional televison. Behaviourism became the name of the game ... Many classroom teachers view the results of all this as a curriculum kaleidoscope ...

The paper argues that professional autonomy has been eroded by the 'Band-Aid approach' to curriculum development, the 'scapegoat approach' of blaming social problems on schools, the 'big brother approach' to controlling funds for support programmes, and 'the accountability approach of blaming teachers for just about everything'. It argues for open discussion of educational policy, and teacher involvement in curriculum change. The NAEP programme is not seen as notably helpful towards this: it reports a NAEP finding of a decline in pupils' political knowledge between 1969 and 1976, and a NAEP press release suggesting that 'citizenship should be added to the three Rs as an equally important basic skill'. It quotes the response of a number of educators, that the present over-emphasis on the three Rs by means of test programmes is the reason for the decline in pupils' knowledge of politics and citizenship.

Evaluation in Retrospect

Accountability is still a rampant political theme in the USA, but the high noon of testing may have come and gone. One unintended and wholly satisfactory result has been to expose the follies of behaviourism, and the limitations of any attempt to reduce educational process to measurable outcomes. The absurdity of such 'psychomotor objectives' as determining eye-hand coordination by the ability of a child to throw a bean bag into a basket 'tilted towards him at a forty-five degree angle and placed four feet in front of him' (Michigan *Common Goals of Education*, 1971) is more widely recognised, although not as yet among the public at large. But two regrettable results have been to obscure the real educational issues, and lower the morale and status of teachers. The real income of teachers has declined, and the pressure of doing a difficult job which is increasingly 'defined by the opinions of others' (Foshay, 1977) undermines self-esteem. Resignations and early retirements are common, often with better-paid jobs in the offing. Recruitment of new graduates from training programmes 'dropped by about forty per cent in the late 1970s' (*Guardian*, 21 July 1980). The same report quotes an employment officer for Los Angeles schools: 'Teaching simply is not as desirable a position as it used to be'. The result is a growing teacher shortage, even for English teachers where two years ago there was a big surplus.

At least one state (Massachussets) has recognised the dangers of indiscriminate testing, and opted for criterion-referenced tests on a random basis 'to measure long-term trends' (Black and Marjoram, 1979). The director of the state bureau of research and assessment 'felt that the minimum competency movement, involving definitions of cut-off points which were arguable and legally actionable, the "public shame" approach to improving schools performance and the narrowing of the aims of education was potentially harmful'.

There are, however, growing doubts among the academic community about assessment in general. Pring and Selby (1980) give an account of a seminar attended by Richard Pring at Stanford University, involving school superintendents and principals and a number of academics originally associated with the development of NAEP. Most had at first supported NAEP, and still admired the technical quality of its exercises:

> But the general feeling was that ... the results did not warrant the time, effort or money spent on this kind of exercise, for the following reasons.

The pursuit of its original aim of monitoring long-term trends did not yield information that was sufficiently significant for any practical purposes ...

In becoming more politically responsive ... it might well be ... no longer able to maintain the relatively neutral role ...

The choice of background variables (socio-economic group, ethnic group etc) could ... reinforce prevailing views about the ineffectiveness of schools against rather unprepossessing social environment ...

The 'service' aspect of NAEP ... had not had much effect ... 'States had bought the promise (of testing) but not the product'

... The research community was very critical of NAEP, not because of its technical achievements ... but because of its inappropriateness to research questions and decisions

Earlier insistence upon a variety of testing procedures ... had given way to multi-choice paper and pencil tests ... Alternative forms of testing could not be so easily standardised, and the results therefore were seen to be unreliable

What initially were promoted as criterion-referenced tests had in effect become norm-referenced tests, and in that way were in danger of setting standards ...

Criticism of American approaches to national and local testing had, indeed, been mounting throughout the seventies. Stake (1976) argued that 'relevant school evaluation' was more a matter of case study than 'the impressiveness of a highly statistical report'. 'We dare not start with the idea of what it is we can test for, or even what are our goals. Relevant evaluation requires starting with what it is that the teaching and learning are'. In 1973, House noted that the managerial model of evaluation meets a longing for 'a unifying authority that will restore order', and promises greater efficiency. But:

Experience with federal programmes the last decade would indicate the opposite. None of the highly centralised and massive evaluation schemes has worked ... Aggregating problems into massive centralised piles does not solve them ... Most results are never used. Test scores are collected and forgotten. The honest administrator admits that he wants data to impress the public ... [But] no matter how hard one tries, in comparative testing fifty per cent will always be below average.

A revealing insight into teacher life in test-dominated schools comes from the case studies which make up part of a detailed survey of the state of science teaching, funded by the National Science Foundation.

This CSSE project (Case Studies in Science Education, Stake and Easley, 1977) found that, nationally, 'science education was being given low priority, yielding to increasing emphasis on basic skills (reading and computation)'. A case study of a school system at Houston, Texas (Denny, 1977) notes that 'Again and again, teachers new to the profession commented on their dismay when the "paperwork of teaching" confronted them: the forms, legal and administrative record keeping'. As a result of accountability pressures, frequent phone calls are made to parents by teachers anxious to interpret test scores: 'Every morning, afternoon, lunch period, preparation period and between periods. Calls, calls, calls.' At a junior high school, 'Friday was test day ... Each subject has a day of the week reserved for testing'. Many teachers' comments show a resigned bitterness about the system:

> You can shut anyone up with a test score: a parent, a superintendent, another teacher

> Scores, scores. Too much emphasis on them ... Lower-level kids fail tests but know much more than we can test

> Accountability is what is on my mind when I give out the grades. If the teachers gave all 'A's the administration would be very happy. They are much more concerned about how parents think we are doing than about how we are doing

> How about a parent competency test?

> Accountability is aimed at the bad teacher but it will miss him and hit the good one clean between the eyes.

This chapter has outlined the extent to which the concept of teacher, school, programme and pupil evaluation has taken root in the USA, where the soil was already well prepared. No such testing tradition exists in the UK, but it is now necessary to examine attempts to import the tradition and apply it to the British education system.

NOTES

1 **Behaviourist.** Behaviourist psychology originated in America in 1913 from the work of J. B. Watson. It studies only what is observable, and preferably what is measurable. It aims to avoid subjective states and notions, like concentration, consciousness and intuition. From experiments on animals in controlled environments, observing measurable responses to applied stimuli, it applies similar concepts and techniques to the be-

haviour of people and purports to solve problems which are defined in these terms. Behaviourists argue that their work is objective, and will ultimately yield general laws of behaviour; against this, it is argued that their problems are artificial, cloaked in elaborate jargon and irrelevant to the actual thought and activities of people.

2 **NAEP.** The National Assessment of Educational Progress was set up in 1967 in the USA to produce the sort of information from national monitoring which might help social policy decisions at federal level. It was organised and administered by the Education Commission of the States (ECS), but under contract to the federal government to devise a suitable test programme. ECS is a non-profit making interstate commission. Since 1978, the work of NAEP has come under greater federal control, and in 1979 the US government made further changes which mean that responsibility for the NAEP testing programme is open to competitive tender every four years. These closer links between national assessment and government policy may become particularly significant under President Reagan.

3 The English Response: The Assessment of Performance Unit

Until 1972, national monitoring of pupils' attainment was a quite insignificant part of the English educational scene. Four-yearly surveys of reading standards at age eleven and fifteen had been conducted since 1948 by the NFER on behalf of the government, and up to 1964 these recorded a steady improvement in test scores. These were the post-war years of steady economic growth and full employment, but by the mid-sixties it became clear that substantial changes in personal and social behaviour were emerging. Teenagers were developing their own sub-culture, based on pop music; most homes acquired a television set, and the new medium reported on the changing scene and itself generated further change.

The effect was to question conventions and open up new opportunities, and the climate was favourable to the growth of comprehensive reorganisation. Until the mid-sixties, ministers of education like Boyle and Crosland spoke of educational issues in much the same terms, despite party differences. But the pace of change brought an inevitable reaction, and by 1969 it was clear that the two parties were moving away from the central ground and polarising policies on social issues like welfare and education around party dogma. In 1969 the first 'Black Paper'[1] on education appeared, and argued that overhasty reorganisation and undue respect for 'progressive' theories had caused a decline in standards. Similar views were a feature of the American scene, and the return of a Conservative administration in 1970 plainly presaged a more questioning attitude towards the work of schools.

In the same year, the NFER conducted its next four-yearly survey, using the same ancient tests — one twenty-three, the other sixteen years old. Testing words like 'mannequin' and 'haberdashery' had little relevance to the post-Beatles era, but when the results were published in 1972, they were seized on as hard evidence of declining standards. The fall in mean scores was very slight, but it was enough. It was a political windfall, and the Secretary of State (Mrs Thatcher) lost no time in establishing, under Sir Alan (now Lord) Bullock, a Committee of Inquiry into 'all aspects of teaching the use of English'. The terms of reference specifically queried the extent to which 'arrangements for monitoring the general level of attainment in these skills can be introduced or improved', and the Committee began by examining the evidence of the reading surveys. After listening to the conflicting interpretations offered by researchers, it found that it was 'not easy to make accurate assessment of the results of such surveys', and decided that 'It is extremely difficult to say whether or not standards of written and spoken English have fallen'. (Bullock, 1975)

One possible conclusion might have been that interpretation problems will blight *all* attempts to monitor language performance over time: instead, Bullock rose to the bait dangled in its terms of reference, and confidently concluded:

> It seems to us beyond question that standards should be monitored, and that this should be done on a scale which will allow confidence in the accuracy and value of the findings ... It must present a comprehensive picture of the various skills that constitute literacy.

Monitoring, it seemed, was not inherently problematic. It was simply a matter of the right technology: 'What is required ... is an instrument that combines practicability with a more comprehensive and therefore more realistic sampling of the skills'. An item bank was the recommended device, along with annual 'light sampling'. So firmly did the Committee endorse the virtues of monitoring as a matter 'beyond question' that the need for 'a system of monitoring' was the first of its principal recommendations.

The Bullock Committee first sat in 1972, and its report was signed in September 1974. It is clear that its views on what it saw as the uncontroversial proposal to extend monitoring must have been settled during 1973. The Committee's secretary was an HMI, following usual practice, and the DES would therefore be well informed as to the progress of its deliberations. In any event, the blueprint for a unit to monitor school performance must have been worked out in the DES by this time. It is the business of civil servants to prepare for contingencies, and the academics appointed by the DES to advise it on research questions would have apprised it of American developments. The NAEP organisation had begun testing in 1967, and the cry of 'back to basics' was already being exploited by some Conservatives. Furthermore, national monitoring extends national control. The DES had demonstrated its control of the public examination system in 1970, when the Schools Council's scheme to run a twenty-point grading system at GCE A-level was turned down by Mrs Thatcher. If there was to be a monitoring unit, the DES would be keen to ensure that, unlike NAEP, control was a direct responsibility of the DES itself. The thinking of the Bullock Committee must have been a great tonic to those planning the new unit: the proposals could now be dusted down and plugged into the political machine at the earliest opportunity.

The APU Takes Wing

Accounts of the evolution of the APU have been given by Simon (1979) and Lawton (1980). My concern is with issues of evaluation rather than political control, and I shall therefore focus my attention on the key moves. A difficulty facing any attempt to analyse DES[2] activities is the Official Secrets Act, which all who work for it must sign. We have seen how various DES-sponsored missions have been free to report the opinions of American government officials: but inquirers at the DES must make do with the cold shoulder. The DES is, it seems, regarded by ambitious civil servants as the billet of the least successful, and this may explain its fear of exposing policy to the public gaze. Its covert ways have been censured twice: in 1975 by the OECD (Organisation for Economic Cooperation and Development) in its *Report on Educational Development Strategy in England and Wales*, and in 1976 by Parliament, in the *Tenth Report of the Expenditure Committee on Policy Making in the Department of Education and Science*. In 1980, the chairman of the Commons Select Committee on Education asked the senior chief inspector of the HMI what advice the HMI had given the minister regarding his decision to close the Centre for Educational Disadvantage: but the minister (Mr Carlisle) 'intervened to try to prevent her answering the question', and so her answer was, 'I'm afraid I cannot answer' (*Education*, 25 July).

This episode bears on the story of the APU in two ways. First, it displays the historical role of the HMI as answerable directly to the Secretary of State. But so, of course, are all the civil service deputy and under-secretaries and other bureaucratic cogs. The HMI, though, are essentially educators and mainly former teachers, while the others are administrators. How are policy conflicts resolved, when educational considerations must be weighed against the wishes of the legislature? Occasionally, a ripple on the surface reveals the struggle beneath it, and throws a ray of light on the question. Thus, when in 1980 the DES published its somewhat reactionary *Framework for the School Curriculum*, a much more liberal statement (*A View of the Curriculum*) followed from the HMI in a matter of hours.

Second, the Centre for Educational Disadvantage (CED) and the APU are, rather surprisingly, political blood brothers. Both saw the light of day in 1974 in order to further the concerns of disadvantaged pupils. But while the CED is now seen as an expendable quango, the APU continues to attract substantial (but secret) funds. The reason for this common parentage is that the first opportunity the DES had to launch the APU as an arm of government came in the White Paper *Educational Disadvantage and the Educational Needs of Immigrants*, published in August 1974. A few months earlier, the education minister in the newly-formed Labour administration (Reg Prentice, later a minister in the 1979 Conservative administration) had mentioned the intention to set up a unit to assess performance in a speech to a teachers' conference. By this time, the Bullock Report, with its *carte blanche* endorsement of monitoring, would have been completed but not yet published. Its publication only a month after the White Paper gave further political reinforcement to the establishment of the new unit.

There was certainly something disingenuous, though, about the manner of its birth. The White Paper is concerned, as one would expect, to 'identify individual children who are suffering from educational disadvantage', and calls for detailed study of:

> the extent to which it is feasible to measure the attainment of boys and girls at school, and differences in that attainment between those suffering from social disadvantage, and others, and between immigrants and others.

The APU could have been mentioned at this point, but instead any reference to such a unit is kept out of the White Paper proper, and confined to Annex A. This gives details of the 'Educational Disadvantage Unit', which will provide for 'all those suffering from educational disadvantage'. In order to do this, a further new unit will be needed to help develop 'relevant criteria' to improve the identification of disadvantaged children, and help allocate resources to meet their interests. This new unit is the Assessment of Performance Unit, and we are directed to Annex B for details of its terms of reference. Here at last, on the final page of the document, is the statement of its aims and tasks (these are given in Chapter 2). And we suddenly learn that identifying 'the incidence of under-achievement' is not, as we had thought, the sole purpose of the new unit, but is in addition to 'the development of methods of assessing and monitoring the achievement of children at school' and identifying 'significant differences of achievement related to the circumstances in which children learn'. Under-achievement is now a subordinate concern: what matters is 'assessing and monitoring' in general.

And yet, it seems doubtful whether this elaborate yet quite transparent way of shuffling the APU on to the stage in carpet slippers really fooled anyone. Within months (July 1975) the DES had been obliged to write to the teacher unions, confirming that the APU 'will be concerned with the wider subject of the developing of methods of assessing the performance of children generally, of which the problems of under-achievement form only a part'. Certainly the DES was wary of union reaction, but by late 1974, with a sustained press campaign under way to vilify the work of schools, the unions had seen some advantage for themselves in the new unit. A union official told me in 1980 that

> At that stage, pressure for public statements on performance was inevitable. The APU gave us a base for presenting alternatives to employers' and newspapers' assessments. The papers were very annoyed when the first primary survey results finally came out — there was so little they could pick on. The APU didn't come as a surprise — we always saw it as what it was, not just as something to do with educational disadvantage.

Public combat between power groups tends to have a ritualised aspect: deals are done behind the rhetoric, and political pressure made the APU look like a useful insurance policy both for the DES and for the unions. Even so, there were two significant omissions from the APU's terms of reference which would have raised union suspicions. First, there was no mention of standards. This is one of the most potent words in the unscrupulous politician's vocabulary, and can open up the royal road to minimum competency testing (at that time imminent in the USA), performance contracting (another American innovation, quickly dropped when it became clear that the contractors were simply teaching the answers to the tests), and — an evocative scar on the folk memory of English teachers — payment by results. It *looked* as if the APU would simply collect data — but in what light would the data be presented?

The second omission was any policy statement about the connection between monitoring and the curriculum. The Bullock Report saw monitoring as a response *to* the curriculum, not an effect *on* it: 'The monitoring instruments should be responsive to developments in the curriculum and should avoid setting up "backwash" effects on the teaching in schools'. But what was the APU view on curriculum backwash? The effect of testing on the curriculum was widely recognised: in 1964, for instance, a report of the Mathematical Association on transfer from primary to secondary schools found that

> The replies of LEAs showed wide recognition of the backwash effect of eleven-plus arithmetic papers. The implication is that coaching for examination questions is encouraged at the expense of teaching the pupil to think.

Yet the APU had, as one of its tasks, the promotion of assessment 'in cooperation with LEAs and teachers'. The unions would cooperate with the APU in return for some influence on its policies on these issues.

These negotiations proceeded during 1975, but meanwhile the APU had begun work. (The DES officially declares 1975 as the APU's year of birth, but the secret DES Yellow Book[3] (Lawton, 1980) dates it from August 1974.) In June 1975 the key statement of APU policy appeared, but once again in disguised form. The charade this time was played out in the pages of the august DES house journal, *Trends in Education*. The article was entitled 'Monitoring pupils' progress', and appeared to be a discussion paper. Its author, Brian Kay, was merely 'an HMI at present associated with the work of the APU'. Kay was in fact already the first head of the unit, working alongside a 'Coordinating Group' (known, perhaps appropriately, as COG) of seventeen members, the majority being HMI or DES officials. The others (teachers, academics, administrators) were evidently window dressing, too few to allay union fears or resist DES intentions. In any event, COG's role was to support, not obstruct. This is clear from a letter to me (Dawson, 1980) from the administrative head of the APU:

> This group (COG) never had day-to-day control of the unit as you supposed; this has always been, and will continue to be, the responsibility of the Department ... The original function of the Coordinating Group was to provide advice to the then Head of the Unit on the assessment model to be adopted and the related committee structure.

Of the two academics on COG, one was Dr Clare Burstall, deputy director of the NFER which stood to gain substantially from the national use of tests. The other, Professor John Eggleston, was later to

write a panegyric to the APU and the curriculum benefits it would
bestow:

> The more efficient the measurement — and APU looks set to be very
> efficient — the more influential it is likely to be. The members of
> APU and its committees know that decisions on test content could
> have an impact on what teachers will teach ... It will be a tragedy if ...
> we miss one of the greatest ... opportunities to achieve fundamental
> enhancement of the schooling of our children. (Eggleston, 1978)

The model of assessment advanced by Kay in his 1975 article also
had some disturbing aspects. The first paragraph links the assessment of performance with 'anxiety about standards', and we are told
that 'the administrator needs objective evidence'. The Bullock Report is quickly wheeled out to support monitoring 'to as sophisticated
an extent as possible', as is a paper by an administrator on educational   management,   advocating   monitoring   as   a   'tool   of
management'. Even the eleven-plus examination has, we learn, been
criticised 'not wholly deservedly': it imposed a curriculum backwash
'unnecessarily', not inevitably, and it would have helped if the tests
could have been shown to be 'reliable indicators of the pupils' overall
attainment'. The emphasis has switched from monitoring performance to establishing standards, and a technocratic approach to
testing will, it appears, put everything to rights.

The aim of Kay's model is nothing less than 'to evaluate a curriculum rather than the parts of a curriculum', and this must take account of 'the needs and expectations of society'. Given this instrumental emphasis, Kay urges the assessment not of timetabled
subjects but of 'lines of development' showing the acquisition of 'a
number of skills and items of knowledge' and development 'in a
number of different ways'. There is also the implication, in discussing the eleven-plus examination, that provided the *overall* curriculum effects are measured, any curriculum backwash that occurs
will be wholly desirable. This argument is not entirely explicit, since
to acknowledge it would be to acknowledge that monitoring produces
backwash. But it was later to become important. Kay goes on to suggest six distinct lines of development: by assessing pupil performance
in each, a cross-curricular model will be established which would
leave room for 'the wide diversity ... embodied in school subjects'.
The six lines are: verbal, mathematical, scientific, ethical, aesthetic,
and physical. In each, the items tested should be 'the most significant', although Kay recognises the difficulty of this, and also of iso-
lating these items from a 'context of knowledge'. He asks: 'Is it, how-

ever, possible to assess the degree to which the aims are being met without dictating content?' The paper's optimistic mood might induce us to think that the answer is yes, given 'the widest possible range of modes of assessment'. Again, technology will, by implication, step in and solve what are seen as merely technical problems.

Finally, Kay specifies how the assessment should be done. Both teachers and pupils should be, surprisingly, 'active participating agents in the assessments'; it should cover 'a broad spectrum of educational objectives'; methods should be 'not restricted to paper and pencil tests'; interpretation of the findings should be 'a strictly professional matter'; a sampling process 'will be all that is required'; and a desirable by-product would be testing materials to 'help in the purely internal assessment procedures of schools'.

Kay's paper at no point mentions the APU by name, and neither is there any reference to the educationally disadvantaged; the White Paper has been left far behind. But then, there is no reason to suppose that Kay's article is the entire APU blueprint; on the contrary, these are only 'preliminary thoughts ... My purpose is more to initiate discussion than to suggest solutions'. The paper ends, though, with a warning:

> The alternative (to a comprehensive monitoring system) could prove to be a growing pressure for the imposition of far cruder measures of educational effectiveness that could both restrict the freedom of the teacher ... and distort the work of schools through the application of far less adequate criteria of performance.

Kay is raising the spectre of minimum competency testing, which was now looming over the American scene. But his paper is more than a political response, which may have been all the DES wanted: it shows an educational commitment to monitoring, and a desire to make curriculum sense of it. Two years later, another group of HMI were to publish *Curriculum 11-16* (1977), a collection of papers arguing, like Kay's, for a view of the whole curriculum. It should 'be concerned with introducing pupils during the period of compulsory schooling to certain essential "areas of experience"'. Although this appeared after the 'great debate' and Green Paper, it had been 'overtaken by events': it was, in other words, not the direct result of these events but of earlier discussion. There is a close similarity between Kay's six lines of development, and the eight areas, which are: the aesthetic and creative; the ethical; the linguistic; the mathematical; the physical; the scientific; the social and political; the spiritual. The last two, in Kay's formulation, have been subsumed under the ethical, and this was later to be re-christened 'personal and social development'. In this light, the APU looks like a contrivance to introduce a certain style of common curriculum by means of the backwash from monitoring. Certainly the two groups must have been meeting at the same time, during 1974 and 1975, and must have been aware of each other's ideas; and both are offering a decoction of Hirst's forms of knowledge and understanding, first outlined ten years earlier (Hirst, 1965). But to see one as the agent of the other is probably to presume more art and subtlety than can be found in organisations like the DES.

But the cloak and dagger style favoured by the APU fosters such speculations, and by 1976 some device was needed to allow the APU's activities to be given wider consideration. The first working group, on language, had already been established in 1975, having been given a fair wind by the Bullock Report. And in 1975 the NFER† had published *Tests of Attainment in Mathematics in Schools* (TAMS) — the fruits of a research project commissioned by the DES, and in advance of the establishment of the APU. This is further evidence that the APU was no sudden inspiration. The NFER had collected a £305 000 grant to develop language tests, and was obviously well placed to collect the mathematics contract. Its position within the APU was by now further reinforced, since a Statistics Advisory Group had been set up within the APU, and of its ten members, four were HMI, one a DES nominee, and three from the NFER. It is interesting that the only two outsiders, Professors Goldstein and Nuttall, have been severe critics of the APU testing strategy (Goldstein and Blinkhorn, 1977; Nuttall 1979).

In March 1976 Brian Kay and Clare Burstall spent three weeks in the USA, looking at national and local testing. The following month the APU acquired an advisory committee, in addition to the Coordinating Group (COG) and the specialist groups on statistics and language. The new group was called the Consultative Committee (CON, perhaps significantly, in DES jargon) and was once again made up of invited members. Four are academics; eight are from local authorities; twelve are from teachers' organisations, and seven represent other interests to do with education (total, thirty-one). Until 1980, CON had no written terms of reference. Now each member has individual terms of reference, which make it clear that CON has no executive responsibility whatever. Also, members of CON are now invited to serve for a fixed term only. A member of CON has told me:

Burstall and Kay were persuaded in the US that it was necessary to talk to teachers to make the APU work. The Consultative Committee was meant to be a talking shop by the DES, run by the Coordinating Group. But we were not just prepared to discuss papers — we wanted to take a view.

The official reason for the long delay in establishing CON was difficulty in finding a chairman (the first chairman, Professor Barry Supple, was replaced by Professor John Dancy from September 1980). It seems more likely that the DES dithered for a long while on the necessity for CON, and the unions certainly pressed for adequate representation. Meanwhile, the APU expanded. By October 1976 the APU working group on mathematics had met, and within months the contract (worth £403 000) had gone to the NFER. The APU had become a big spender; little wonder that, in a perhaps unguarded aside, Black and Marjoram (1979) could remark, 'NAEP clearly envied the more extended funding commitments upon which the APU was able to work'.

In early 1977 the DES published a 'programme of work' for the APU, written by Kay as its head. There is again no mention of the educationally disadvantaged, and fresh prominence is given to making the assessment materials developed through the APU's agency 'available (with suitable safeguards) to other users, such as LEAs'. The emphasis on monitoring standards rather than on testing as an instrument of diagnosis is now quite overt. By now the political climate had changed. Mr Callaghan's Ruskin College speech in the autumn of 1976 committed the government to curriculum intervention, for the first time since the 1935 Regulations for Secondary Schools. It was followed by the DES agenda document for the 'great debate' on education, and this document justifies the establishment of the APU in 1974 (not 1975!) as the result of 'recognition that further work was needed on sampling standards' (*Educating Our Children*, DES 1977). When the Green Paper appeared in July 1977, considerable space was allotted to 'standards and assessment'. The APU, though, appeared under the sub-heading 'pupils as individuals', and the notion that schools should be judged by 'basic tests of numeracy and literacy' was firmly rejected. It looks as if the DES had at last seen the dangers of tying the APU too explicitly to standards; by now the worst excesses of the American MCT movement were plain to see. But the virtues of testing as an aspect of professionalism are firmly embraced; formal evaluation techniques are seen as a part of teaching life, linked to the APU by LEA testing programmes using the same evaluative language:

A number of education authorities have already decided on or are considering monitoring the performance of pupils in their areas: tests suitable for this purpose are likely to come out of the work of the APU. Here again the Department's concern is that there should be consistency within local education authorities and wherever possible between authorities.

It was now time for Kay to be moved off the APU, and in January 1977 another HMI, Tom Marjoram, took over as head. In 1979, Marjoram was to declare lyrically that:

> The Green Paper pointed us toward a system in which the individual process of every child is properly and regularly assessed by his teachers ... in which classroom, LEA and national assessment are comparable and interrelatable ... In this endeavour, the APU is proud to play its part.

The technology of assessment is now in full flower: like the computer-coded parts of motor cars, children move forward from local workshops to assembly plants and out to the consumers on programmed assembly belts, each child labelled with a row of product code numbers and each fulfilling its measured destiny in the grand design. As Kay departed, he might justly have considered that in three years he had taken the APU from nothing to a major political presence in the DES and in the whole education system. Furthermore, it looked as if his original concept of the APU was firmly established, in three important respects.

First, the *cross-curricular* model appeared secure. Assessing all six lines of development was the cornerstone of Kay's vision of the APU as a *professional* aid. In his American report, NAEP had been criticised for using a model 'leaning heavily towards an analysis in terms of school subjects' (Burstall and Kay, 1978) and if all went well, the APU would avoid this.

Second, care was being taken to give credibility to the APU surveys as a source of *longitudinal data* for *national* planning. The US trip had revealed the negligible use of NAEP data at this level. But Kay's faith in testing was unshaken, and it looked as if the NFER team had found a technical device (to be discussed shortly) which would guarantee the comparative value of the data from year to year.

Third, the US trip had also shown the need to tie the national sample to the tests of *local* authorities: 'If it is to have an influence, it must necessarily be at federal level' (Burstall and Kay, 1978). Hence the need to persuade LEAs to use APU material and so penetrate the schools themselves. The key here was to devise a way of *adapting*

APU tests for the mass market. Again, the NFER appeared to have the answer: the Rasch model would allow an item bank to be established, run by the NFER. This was subsequently set up in July 1977, under the title LEASIB (Local Education Authorities' and Schools' Item Banking Project).

In public pronouncements about the APU, its staff were anxious to confirm that the intention was to minimise any backwash effect on the curriculum. But a telling passage from the first American report shows that the intention was exactly the reverse:

> The lesson for the APU is, we feel, clear if it is to avoid the criticisms levelled against NAEP ... The interests and involvement of those bodies, such as the subject associations, need to be engaged so that they will take advantage of its findings *and use them to further desirable curriculum developments.* (Burstall and Kay, 1978; my italics)

Kay had evidently created a powerful engine for influencing the curriculum. Like the American NAEP, its origins had been linked to the problems of disadvantaged pupils; for in Chapter 2, I pointed out that the first objective of the original NAEP scheme was to obtain data that would locate 'deficiencies and inequalities'. The DES repeated the ruse in launching the APU. But unlike NAEP, the new unit was under its exclusive control: the DES was set to achieve national curriculum control by stealth.

Within months of Kay's departure, however, political and theoretical cracks were to appear in the structure of the APU which undermined all three elements of the model.

The Assault on the Citadel

The first signs of trouble had, in fact, already appeared. At the first meeting of CON in April 1976, Kay's model of six lines of development was presented for rubber-stamping by the new body. It was clear that COG was running the APU on behalf of the DES, and testing in all six areas was to be a *fait accompli.* The language and exploratory mathematics groups were already under way, and an exploratory science group had met as early as 1975 (although this fact does not appear in any public APU documents I have seen). The attempt to foist the six-sided model on to CON was resisted chiefly by the teachers' organisations. Testing in subjects with a basic appeal like English, mathematics and science was one thing; extension to physical development, aesthetic development and personal and social development (PSD) was another. All three seemed to threaten the autonomy of schools, but PSD seemed to threaten the autonomy of pupils: assessing a child's moral and religious beliefs was a whole new dimension.

The next meeting of CON had the impression that the six-sided model had been accepted. Even at the third meeting of CON this distorted view of the range of opinions had to be challenged. The DES argued that if testing were limited to English, mathematics and science, there would be a constraint on the curriculum. This, of course, tacitly acknowledged that there would, after all, be a strong curriculum backwash effect. But the opposition argued that trying to test the other three lines of development would lead to even greater dangers. The DES, however, persisted and exploratory groups in the three controversial areas were set up. The decision to explore PSD testing led to the resignation from CON of Lord Alexander — an under-publicised event, since, as Sir William Alexander, he had been a very influential figure in local authority politics and affairs for a long time. But it was clear that the DES saw exploration as leading to discovery: given the limited powers of CON, PSD testing appeared to be unstoppable. The then Secretary of State (Mrs Shirley Williams) herself attended the next meeting of CON, and the crisis was largely kept under wraps.

Kay's model now came under threat from another direction. Since it purported to assess the whole curriculum, how could it omit two further areas: the first foreign language, and technology? Politically, this pressure was hard to resist, since our membership of the European Economic Community seems to oblige the DES to lay special emphasis on foreign language teaching, and the Callaghan government laid equal emphasis on education as a preparation for industry and a productive economy. So the model was extended to create two more working groups, one of which (foreign language) had, in 1980, got to the stage of publishing a CON-approved testing model. But, of course, the admission of testing in this area destroys the basis of the model, since learning a foreign language is a mere skill and has no place in a model of intellectual development and understanding. Technology, too, is a contentious candidate: how far is it distinctive from the scientific, or the aesthetic?

Meanwhile the PSD group continued to explore its territory, and in the autumn of 1978 its first fruits were presented to what proved to be a 'long, stormy meeting', according to a member of CON. 'If a vote had been taken at that meeting, personal and social development would have been buried there and then.' But at the next meeting of

CON, the PSD group was authorised to keep going despite the continued opposition of teachers' representatives. 'It was the support of the LEA representatives which kept the PSD group going.' In the event, though, the PSD operation was brought to an end, and in curious circumstances. But in 1979 the DES sponsored an American visit specifically to further the PSD inquiries, and advertised for a research assistant to the group. It looked as if its support of PSD assessment was being prosecuted with vigour.

Then, in March 1980, the PSD exploratory group decided to take matters a stage further, and put before CON a consultative document 'mapping the territory', which set out arguments for and against PSD testing. It emphasised that 'mapping the territory is not the same as deciding what is to be assessed', but argued that informed discussion was not possible until the mapping had been done. On PSD assessment, it suggested that 'assessment is no more likely to leave the way open to central direction than the failure to assess'. Certainly the document discusses controversial issues: that is an inescapable part of PSD inquiry. But it is broadly neutral in tone, and simply seeks to publish its classes and categories so that informed discussion of the issues can continue on a public basis. But CON voted not to allow publication of the consultative document, and with that decision APU work into personal and social development came to an abrupt end. (The Schools Council is considering some further work on PSD, but as a curriculum inquiry and not as an aspect of national testing.)

What had gone wrong? The teachers' representatives had opposed the PSD work consistently, and voted against publication as part of their root and branch objection. It would have been surprising had they not voted against the proposal. The critical factor was the decision of at least some LEA representatives to vote against it, despite their previous support of PSD work. It is interesting, too, that a month before the CON meeting, the HMI in charge of the professional work of the APU (John Graham) agreed, in answer to a question at a teachers' conference, that the future of the APU tests 'was uncertain and that the unit had made no commitment to such testing' (*The Times Educational Supplement*, 15 February 1980). Further, a DES official had intimated a few weeks before the meeting to a member of CON known to be opposed to PSD monitoring that 'there was nothing to worry about'.

Since the consultative document put forward by the PSD group was relatively innocuous in the context of the previous CON debate on PSD monitoring, it is difficult to see why the LEA representatives switched from loyal support to outright opposition; the educational arguments were unchanged. The decision must, therefore — like almost everything to do with the APU — have been a political one. It is interesting that this outcome seems to have been expected by the DES, which has done no more than record its disappointment at the result. Certainly the decision to terminate the PSD work finally disposes of Kay's 'lines of development' model.

The other principal criticism of the original APU model appears to be technical in character, but in fact raises important educational questions about the nature of testing. It is to do with the Rasch model, the device chosen by the NFER as a valid way of using the APU data to study longitudinal changes in performance over time, and of tailoring APU-validated tests to LEA and school requirements via the LEASIB project. The need is for *objective information* — Kay's paper called for 'objective evidence' for administrators — which will reflect the actual achievement of individuals rather than the nature of the test itself. Over time, test items date as the culture changes, and so (as with the NFER reading tests) they lose their validity as comments on school performance. The favoured NFER solution to this problem is to use a model of a testing instrument which appears to allow for adjustment over time, and then to ensure that what is tested conforms with this model: 'The criterion is that items should fit the model, and not that the model should fit the items'. This is worrying in itself, but so also is the Rasch model chosen (named after G. Rasch, a Danish mathematician). This model assumes, as a mathematical convenience, that the likelihood of a person getting a test item right depends on only one factor (or 'trait' in psychologists' jargon), and so can be represented as a *single number.* Thus the chance that a child will get an answer right in an English test depends only on some generalised 'English ability': furthermore, the model assumes that by means of this single number all the items in a test can be arranged in order of difficulty, and that this difficulty order will *stay the same* regardless of who takes the test, the different ways in which they have been taught, their different cultural backgrounds or whatever. This seems to be a fairly preposterous assumption, and one which should not be allowed to stray outside a test technician's laboratory.

But the NFER's researchers have advocated the use of this model in designing and analysing the APU tests in language and mathematics, and particularly in connection with the LEASIB project, which revolves around item banks containing 'a large collection of test questions' (NFER leaflet, 1979). The Rasch model offers the promise of an absolute scale of testing, ranking all individuals on a single scale so that tests can be switched between different times and circumstances but all calibrated to the same base line. And if the base line is made to coincide with that of the national APU tests, then the owners of the item bank can claim to offer tests which tie school or LEA assessment direct to national norms. This is the NFER's stated aim for LEASIB:

> With the permission of the DES it is intended that the Project item banks will be constructed in such a way that results obtained using tests designed for LEA survey purposes will be broadly compatible with the performance measures presented in the APU reports.

A further reason for the NFER's commitment to the Rasch model is that, at first sight, it appears to solve the problem of longitudinal stability. If an item is considered dated, as in the NFER reading test example of outmoded words like 'haberdashery' and 'mannequin', a more appropriate item can be inserted with the same difficulty level — the same number to represent the chance of getting it right — and so the validity of the test is guaranteed over time. But Goldstein (1979) has argued that the relative difficulties between items on the Rasch model will change over time, since the only meaning that can be attached to an item is the single mathematical concept of its difficulty value. As time passes, the relative difficulties will change as a result of contextual factors. Suppose that in 1979, an item using fractions appears to be easier than one using decimals: then this defines the relative difficulty of the two items and, if the model is to work as the NFER and APU intend, this relative difficulty must stay constant. But in 1984, pupils may well find the decimal item less difficult, relative to the fractions item, than five years before. Metrication is increasing, and the backwash effect of the APU tests themselves might cause a change in teaching emphasis of this kind. It follows that the 1984 results will be incompatible with those five years earlier, because of the inability of the Rasch model to cope with the change of relative item difficulty levels over time:

> Despite its claim, the methodology of objective measurement contributes nothing to the resolution of the difficulties facing test constructors ... and offers over-simple solutions to complex problems ... The one thing which is not revealed clearly by those who advocate the methodology, however, is just what the mathematics implies in educational terms. (Goldstein, 1979)

Talk of 'objective tests' and sophisticated statistical models conceals the real issues — the educational value judgments on which the validity of the whole assessment programme depends.

Criticism of the Rasch model has grown since 1977, and the long-term usefulness of the APU results must now be in doubt on this score alone. Equally, the future of the NFER LEASIB project is threatened although efforts may be made to paper over the cracks. At this stage, it will be helpful to review the testing so far carried out by the APU and the problems that have already been exposed.

The Tested Subjects: English, Mathematics and Science

There are no immediate prospects of systematic APU testing beyond the three areas of English, mathematics and science. It is clear that tests in just these three subjects present a very partial view of performance in the entire curriculum: neither, indeed, has it proved possible to retain the original concept of the 'lines of development' in working out the tests. It is the three school subjects which are being tested. Despite the intention to avoid a 'school timetable' model, the grand design has crumbled and the result so far is a much more diminished model of the curriculum than the ten areas of the NAEP scheme scorned in the APU American report (Burstall and Kay, 1978). In order to see how the actual business of devising tests has mutilated the original intentions, it is necessary to look at each area in turn.

Language

Historically, the case for language testing had already been established before the APU was set up. Given the Bullock Report's unqualified support for 'more information than has ever been available before', the language working party had a mandate for testing on the grand scale. Yet of the four modes of language activity identified by Bullock — reading, writing, listening and speaking — the problems of monitoring listening and speaking were quickly set aside, not least because 'it would be difficult to establish comparability across time' (*Language Performance*, APU, 1978). But the group was undaunted: it would provide 'solid information' instead of 'purely subjective judgment'. At once there is the false promise that by testing pupils, value issues are suddenly set aside and the technical apparatus will take over. It was recognised, though, that testing brought dangers:

> While the whole APU monitoring exercise has been deliberately de-
> signed to minimise any 'backwash' on the curriculum, it must be ac-
> cepted that assessment procedures may transmit messages to teachers
> about curricular priorities. Accordingly, it is essential for the APU to
> produce national forms of assessment that do justice to the intuitive
> model of writing acted on by most teachers.

However, the group's aim of monitoring 'a wide range of reading and
writing tasks' led them to hope that 'the monitoring process will not
be something divorced from the learning process, but rather a con-
tribution to it'. If this means anything, it seems to imply a wish to use
the APU tests as a way of fostering 'language across the curriculum'.
At the least, it acknowledges that the monitoring process cannot be
'neutral' or curriculum-proof: as soon as you make an observation,
you distort the process you are trying to observe.

In the event, the first APU field testing to be carried out was of
mathematics. Testing of English (or 'language', as it is rather grandly
described) only began in 1979, and the official survey report was
delayed until May 1981. But the draft report on the testing of eleven-
year-olds was leaked to the press, and the results appeared to confirm what any informed observer would expect. But the promise of
'solid information' was scarcely fulfilled: the expensive research has
brought us no nearer a definition of literacy, and neither could it: instead, we must rely on statements like 'more than ninety-six per cent
have attained sufficient mastery of writing, spelling and punctuation
to make what they write understood on first reading' (*The Times
Educational Supplement*, 25 July 1980). There is the unsurprising
news that eleven-year-old girls are better than boys not only at reading (as everyone knew) but also at writing (as every teacher also
knew): and a collection of trivial statements, like 'more girls preferred
long, thick books, while more boys stated a preference for short
books'. The whole elaborate exercise has produced either the obvious, the unimportant, or the misleading: for example, the result
that reading test scores got worse as staffing ratios improved is unin-
terpretable as it stands: it conflicts with common sense and may be
due to a variety of circumstances. Monitoring has not clarified the
issues, but confused them.

What is much more interesting, however, is some evidence concerning the school impact of the tests themselves. A perceptive article
by a junior school head (Carter, 1980) reveals his dismay at the nature of the test tasks administered to his pupils: the reading tests were
'rather dull passages, not dissimilar to those found in the comprehension textbooks'. Another task presented pupils with 'a long, dead-

ly boring passage about fireworks' taken, it appeared, from an en-
cyclopaedia. The children were to use this information to make notes
and then 'write about a firework they know'. Carter points out that
this kind of teaching strategy is widely discredited, and cannot become part of the child's 'action knowledge' because it has no connection with his concrete experiences. In devising such tests, the
APU testers 'encourage and give official support to practices which
many of us consider to be bad'. Carter had complained to the head of
the NFER language team, only to be told that 'the majority of head
teachers and their children approved of the language testing materials
of the APU'. But this, as Carter points out, does not justify bad practice.

What gives this article particular significance is that it drew a reply
from Douglas Barnes (*The Times Educational Supplement*, 1 August
1980), a member of the APU language steering group from the
beginning and the author of a number of books on the teaching of
English. Barnes is sympathetic to Carter's position about the backwash effect of the APU tests: 'these are fears I share'. He accepts,
too, Carter's 'teacherly concern' that schooling should engage with
children's 'first-hand concerns'. But 'it is in the nature of any national test that such particular experiences cannot be easily tapped',
although writing tasks set in the tests 'can undoubtedly be
improved'. Barnes admits that he

> joined the language advisory committee in the hope of helping to make
> tests that did not too much misrepresent the nature of reading and
> writing, and found with some relief that many other members of the
> various committees felt similar anxieties about possible harm that
> might be done.

Barnes is at pains to distinguish between the 'influences which are
likely to be inherent in any kind of national monitoring' and 'the particular tasks used': he accepts that all monitoring is harmful, but justifies his decision to take part in the APU's work on the grounds that
he might then at least be able to minimise these harmful effects. And
the testing would go ahead anyway, since 'the establishment of the
APU was a political decision made originally by a Labour government and now sustained by a Conservative one'. But, of course, the
decision to advocate national monitoring of language performance
was not, in the first instance, political; it was an overwhelming
recommendation of the Bullock Committee, which considered the
educational arguments to be 'beyond question'.

It now begins to look as if the enthusiasm of the English establishment for national monitoring is on the wane, and certainly

Barnes's letter shows that thoughtful members of the APU committees are 'acutely concerned' about the dangers to which it leads. And one must, of course, respect the view that if testing is inevitable, taking part in the process is a way of influencing it. But the dangers, cannot be eliminated by improving the technology of testing; they are absolutely implicit in the nature of testing itself.

Mathematics

The first APU monitoring report to be published came out in 1980 (*Primary Survey Report No 1*, APU). It had a head start because the NFER team developing the tests 'used the work of the TAMS project as its starting point' (*Monitoring Mathematics*, APU 1978). The TAMS materials appeared in 1975 and, with hindsight, it is clear that the DES saw this piece of research as a discreet dry run for the basic APU operation. The report of the NFER TAMS team disclosed that deciding on the assessment topics was far from clear cut — 'agreement or consensus was difficult to obtain'. Practical tests were included, and have been retained in the APU tests. The validity of the TAMS tests, and the problems of item-bank sampling so as to ensure a representative balance of questions, have been criticised by Leonard (1977). The most telling comments on the APU tests themselves have been made by teachers (Cording *et al.*, 1980). The assessment model lists thirteen sub-categories for the eleven-year-old's mathematics curriculum: money, time, weight, temperature; length, area, volume, capacity; shapes, lines, angles; symmetry, transformations, coordinates; rate, ratio and proportion; generalised arithmetic; sets and relations; data representation; and five to do with the concepts of number and computations with them. One teacher points out that this list 'could become accepted as a common curriculum in maths ... There is ... the danger that ... the content becomes accepted automatically, rather than being treated as problematic and having its assumptions carefully analysed'.

This is a particular danger since, as another teacher remarks, 'the national pattern in the APU report does not appear to reflect the aims of, and the range of, mathematics defined in the HMI document *Mathematics 5-11, A Handbook of Suggestions*'. And yet 'The APU survey provides a baseline. The begging question is: "Is the baseline too low or too high?" The APU passed no comment'. A general criticism of the APU report is that it consists mainly of statistical information: it seems to go to great lengths to avoid interpreting the data it presents. Equivalent NAEP reports go beyond the bare facts and use a panel of experts to offer an interpretation and give more information on what pupils seem capable of doing. Yet Kay's visit to NAEP led him to stress that the APU's findings should be 'of interest and concern to the teacher' (Burstall and Kay, 1978). But interpretation means value judgments, and so conflicts with the neutral stance to which the APU is formally committed. If, like NAEP, it were not a government agency, it need not be shackled so firmly to bald statement and the techniques of number crunching.

Another point raised by a teacher is of importance: 'Were the tests in fact testing mathematical ability? It is possible that ... the ability to comprehend the written part of the question is what is really being assessed'. This issue had come to prominence as a result of a question which asked children to work out a cricketer's batting average, having been told to divide 'the number of runs scored by the number of times out'. The question tests the same operation as another, which told pupils there were eighteen squares in a bar of chocolate, with six in each row, and asked how many rows there were. But while eighty-three per cent got this right, only twenty-five per cent got the right answer for the batting average. Does this, though, support the report's contention that there is

> a fairly sharp decline in performance as pupils' understanding of the concepts is probed more deeply and their basic knowledge has to be applied in more complex settings or unfamiliar contexts

— or does it not confirm what every maths teacher knows: that most of the difficulty with 'problems' is in getting children to acquire the quite advanced skill of converting the abstractions of words into an operation with numbers? The children's poorer score on the batting average question, however, was seized on by sections of the press: one of the few items from an essentially tame report that could be treated in this irresponsible way. But, as House (1973) pointed out, 'Public understanding of test scores is likely to increase public dissension and be unfair to various individuals'.

A second survey of eleven-year-olds was carried out in 1979, and leaked accounts of the draft of the report suggest that, like the first, it will have little to say to teachers. The fact that 'Less than half the pupils knew what a protractor was when shown one' (*The Times Educational Supplement*, 25 July 1980) may well attract publicity, but illustrates again that a stupid question will get a stupid answer. As a secondary mathematics teacher, I would much rather introduce pupils to the use of the protractor at an age when they could get it right than have the wretched task of getting them to unlearn and relearn. As in the first mathematics survey and in the unpublished language survey, there were higher scores when the teacher-to-pupil ratio decreased: but, of course, smaller classes are more commonly found in deprived areas or sleepy country schools — the bare facts are simply misleading. And all the reports show that pupils do better in schools in more affluent areas — a result that will astonish no one.

A third mathematics report was published in September 1980, after earlier press leaks (*The Times Educational Supplement*, 8 February 1980). This gives the results of tests on fifteen-year-olds, and again shows that 'performances varied widely according to how questions were asked', and the order in which they were asked (which weakens the invariant assumptions of the Rasch model). Also, 'many pupils misunderstood the questions', which suggests that all the doubts about whether the tests test mathematics or English are just as valid. It further emerges that, of the pupils tested,

> Only sixty per cent could give the quantity of ingredients needed to make thirty tarts given the quantity that would make twelve. In the primary survey, seventy per cent got a similar question right.

Results like this have been turned up by the NAEP surveys, and invite headlines like 'Children get worse in secondary school'. As it happens, the APU has itself given the answer to this conclusion, in the second American report:

> Another significant point ... was that the sequence of children's learning was not necessarily that of a continuous improvement in competence. For example, research on children's ability to solve problems to do with temperature showed that very young children succeeded, intermediate age children did not succeed and that older children succeeded again: the change is thought to be due to initial success based on operating a rule automatically, later overtaken by confusion as the child struggles to understand, with a subsequent improvement as understanding is achieved. If this is true of many areas then 'snapshots' taken at one particular age need very careful interpretation — regression may be an inevitable part of development (Black and Marjoram, 1979).

In short, we know very little about how children learn — but testing means we can easily jump to wrong conclusions. And the harm done by such false interpretations may damage teacher morale and needlessly lower public esteem for the work of schools.

Two final points must be made about the mathematics results. First, it is clear that what is being tested is not 'mathematics across the curriculum': these are simply tests of what goes on in mathematics lessons. So it is evident that *de facto*, if not yet *de jure*, the original cross-curricular model has been abandoned. Second, it was a cardinal point of the original model that the APU tests should be criterion-referenced, and not purport to define norms by which children's work could be judged. In the Burstall/Kay report, NAEP came in for criticism on this account. But, in fact, what has the APU ended up with? Nothing but a series of statements which in effect define norms of performance. For example, at age fifteen more than eighty per cent could multiply seventy-six by seven; two thirds could divide 1.8 by 3, and so on. Teachers and — in particular — LEAs can use these results to define achievement norms, with the implication that the APU has defined the baseline for numeracy. The fact is that the APU tests are in effect — if not in intention — norm referenced, with all the vices of such tests carefully chronicled by Burstall and Kay.

Science

To testing buffs, the science tests are generally regarded as better executed and intrinsically more interesting than those produced by the NFER for language and mathematics. The cost of the science contract was nearly half a million pounds, shared between research teams at Leeds University and Chelsea College, London. It was not awarded until 1977, and runs for five years. The first science tests were carried out in 1980, and include practical tests. It is clear from the report of the research team on their test design (*Science Progress Report 1977-78*, APU, 1979) that much intellectual effort has gone into tackling difficult questions and hammering out workable or defensible solutions. Theirs is also easily the most informative of all the APU group reports, and the frankest in indicating points of criticism.

The first problem for the science group was to meet Kay's requirement (Kay, 1975) that scientific ability be tested 'without defining the area of information with which the student is expected to be familiar' — that is, to test the *process* of scientific thinking independent of *content*. The problem was perhaps severer in science than in more familiar areas like language and mathematics; obviously, the amount of science content offered to pupils in schools up and down the country will vary a great deal in both degree and kind. It proved impossible to effect this separation, for the fundamental reason that learning and doing science means using concepts, and 'concepts, though in one sense the products of others' inquiries, become a necessary part of the process of inquiring' (Pring, 1979). The science team has therefore been forced to adopt a three-dimensional model defining 'process categories', 'concept areas' and 'contexts'. The three contexts selected are: contexts of science teaching, contexts of teaching in other subjects, and contexts of everyday or out-of-school situations. Six process categories are defined: using symbolic representations, using apparatus and measuring instruments, observation tasks, interpretation and application, design of investigations, and performing investigations.

The notion of 'concept areas' is more controversial, since it is nothing less than the 'content base' for the monitoring operation. It 'represents a consensus as to what is a reasonable concept base for the assessment'. Once again, the original intention to make the APU monitoring a representation of 'things as they are' has had to be ditched, simply because detached observation is impossible. The tester must have some idea of what he is supposed to find, and so the imperative of evaluating performance gives rise to a statement of what one *ought* to find, rather than what is there. The 'concept areas', therefore, amount to a syllabus of basic scientific knowledge. We are told that 'these were examined by many teachers; further amendments were made in the light of their comments'; but plainly the likelihood of curriculum backwash now becomes a near certainty.

At age eleven, for example, no less than thirty-one 'concept statements' are listed. The implication is that if pupils are to do well in the APU tests, this is what they must know. Some of the statements, like 'air fills the space around or near the earth's surface' one might take for granted. But 'substances taken from the soil must be replaced to maintain fertility' must be demonstrated if it is not to be learnt by rote; after all, the value of fertilisers was scarcely discovered in farming until the last century. Teaching a primary-school child factual knowledge of this kind may, or may not, seem an appropriate task for the teacher. Another group of concepts belongs to physics rather than biology: for example, 'the average speed of an object is found by dividing the distance moved by the time taken'. This is in fact a remarkably sophisticated concept, since the idea of average speed is an abstraction which does not occur in everyday experience. Similarly, 'To make anything move ... there has to be a force ... acting on it' is memorised and applied by fifth and sixth formers the world over as Newton's first law, but actually to internalise and understand it is a much more elusive mental condition which eludes many undergraduates. How likely is it that junior school teachers will understand it well enough to teach it usefully to inquiring eleven-year-olds? One might ask, with a professor of science education, 'Do we teach too much physics and teach it too early?' (Elton, 1980). The disturbing thing is that the APU science tests are in effect pre-empting discussion on these issues, which raise fundamental questions to do with the teaching of science and with the educational development of children.

Beyond this baseline of 'concept statements for age 11', the science team has constructed detailed lists of further concepts, arranged in six areas: the interaction of living things with their environment; living things and their life processes; force and field; transfer of energy; the classification and structure of matter; and chemical interactions. These lists are extraordinarily detailed: for instance, under 'living things and their life processes' are the sub-headings: the cell; nutrition; respiration; reproduction; and sensitivity and movement. Under the last sub-heading, three concepts are needed at age 11; four more at age 13; and six more at age 15. It is clear, therefore, that the effect of the APU science monitoring is to define a science programme up to age 16; and, furthermore, it is clear that what is being tested is not science as an aspect of our culture, with unifying concepts cutting across conventional boundaries, but traditional physics, chemistry and biology. It is also by no means self-evident that the researchers' aim of testing the transfer of science concepts from one context to another has any validity: there is no certainty that scientific responses are transferable in this way.

There are, moreover, two further problems which cannot be resolved satisfactorily within the existing framework of the APU operation, but which must be resolved if the results of the tests are to have any real meaning. These are best illustrated by quoting one of the APU sample test items, intended for eleven- and thirteen-year-olds and testing the process category 'performing investigations' and requiring 'concepts which are in the common area of science and mathematics'. The child is given a bottle of water, a large glass jar, a measuring jug, a ruler, a felt tip pen and a paper towel; and told, 'You may not need all of this, because there are different ways of doing this. What you have to do is to find out the volume of your hand (demonstrate cut-off line at wrist)'. The point is, how far is this really a test of science, the scientific method and the grandiose concept 'performing investigations', and how far is it a test of basic reasoning and thinking? In fact, trials of the science tests suggest that what is often being tested is not science skill, but general intelligence. It follows that if the results are to be worth anything in terms of pupils' supposed scientific performance, it is necessary to measure their intelligence in some way so that this factor can be washed out of the results by statistical analysis. But CON has ruled that to use the APU as a cloak for the administration of intelligence tests would be retrograde and politically unacceptable.

This leads to a related problem. The general link between abilities of the kind tested in the science monitoring and the socio-economic background of pupils is well known. In the American NAEP work, asking pupils and teachers direct questions to determine this has been unobjectionable. But it is foreign to English practice, and CON has ruled that while some estimate of home background is important so that this, too, can be allowed for in the results, no pupils or teachers must be asked direct questions about it. The APU is therefore involved in a frenzied 'search for the surrogate', as it is called: a search for some factor which will correlate with home background without the need to ask embarrassing questions. At first it was thought that the take up of school meals by pupils would suffice, but the decline in the service as a result of the Thatcher administration's policies made this non-viable. Currently under investigation is the idea that the better the home background, the more likely the child to do separate science subjects in fourth and fifth year options: then this information could be abstracted from school records.

The APU science team has brought ingenuity to the testing task, but the value of the resulting surveys will depend on what they really mean. The elaborate framework of process and concept factors is the kind of systematic analysis which attracts the admiration of like-minded academics, but its connection with actual pupil learning is entirely speculative and unproven: because, in the nature of things, testing grossly diminishes what it purports to test. A sympathetic Australian visitor to the APU science unit (Brown, 1980) felt bound to point out

> the limitations of an exclusively competency-based, objectives-based approach to testing. The science skills which are definable and the outcomes which are precisely measurable will, I expect, be tested well in the national monitoring. Only a limited attempt is being made to test the less easily definable skills like creative thinking and imaginative reasoning and their less reliably measurable outcomes.

And even the measurable outcomes will be little more than unreliable fodder for speculation if they cannot throw light on why a particular performance level arises. Unless we know why, we can do nothing about it. But this requires information on intelligence and socio-economic factors which may be unobtainable, and arguably ought to be unobtainable.

The APU operation is based on matrix sampling and item banking.

It is to the science team's credit that they will have no truck with the Rasch item banking model favoured by the NFER, and are investigating 'another mathematical model which makes different and somewhat more plausible assumptions. Unfortunately, some of these assumptions cannot readily be put to the test, so it will again be a matter for debate as to whether this model is adequate and more suitable than the Rasch model' (Nuttall, 1979).

The testers' search for objective certainty is a quest for an unattainable goal. As Dr Johnson remarked of an equally bizarre activity, it is not done well; but you are surprised to find it done at all. But while making a dog walk on its hind legs is merely a peculiar diversion, the contrivances of the testers are not merely academic exercises conducted at the taxpayer's expense. They are attempts to reduce a complex and ultimately impenetrable process to measurable outcomes. Inevitably, these attempts present a distorted view of what they claim to measure.

The APU: Has it a Future?

It is a characteristic of pluralist societies — and of educational planning in particular — that it is relatively easy to allow new organisations to come into existence, and almost impossible to get rid of them. As soon as they become institutionalised, their adherents form a political power base and what might at first have come about largely by chance suddenly appears to fulfil an irresistible purpose. Even if some future administration resolved to close down the APU, it would no doubt be argued that such an act would destroy educational standards.

Yet the APU does not deserve to survive. National monitoring has a meretricious attraction, and it has seduced a number of educationists as well as politicians. But at the end of the day its promises prove to be hollow, as American studies of NAEP have at length disclosed:

> Either the change in scores (given an acceptable margin of error) was too small for establishing any trend, *or* the objectives within an area changed too much for comparisons to be made, *or* the objectives monitored, by the time they had been agreed upon by the various bodies concerned, did not represent adequately the variety of pupil achievement. (Pring and Selby , 1980)

To suggest that the activities of the APU and its teams will lead to improved educational activities in schools is — to quote the good doctor again — 'like burning a farthing candle at Dover to shew light at Calais'. If education is to be improved — and there can be no other reason, in truth, for setting up the APU — then the way to do it is not by vain attempts to measure what happens, but by helping teachers to define and solve curriculum problems.

I have argued that the APU has no educational value in its own right and is, indeed, likely to do more harm than good. But this would be an inadequate reason for putting an end to it, since it has considerable political value. To the 1974 Callaghan government, it was a way of fending off Conservative criticism of schools by recourse to the principle that 'if you can't beat 'em, join 'em'. Hence the stress on standards and the rapid growth of APU development groups. To the teachers' organisations, the APU was a risky proposition but a way of countering ill-informed assertion with some sort of facts. Its importance to the Conservative Party is shown by the fact that, of the sixty words devoted to education (under the heading 'standards in education') in the 1979 election manifesto, forty dealt with the APU:

> We shall promote higher standards of achievement in basic skills. The Government's Assessment of Performance Unit will set national standards in reading, writing and arithmetic monitored by tests worked out with teachers and others and applied locally by education authorities.

The APU has clearly come a long way in five short years: from an innocent inquiry into ways of helping disadvantaged pupils, it is seen by the present party of government as its major weapon in a 'back to basics' movement.

Given this emphasis, though, how can one account for the complaisant way in which the DES allowed CON to terminate the work on social and personal development? CON, after all, is only an advisory body. Also, the work on technology, physical and aesthetic development seems to be hanging fire. Although the foreign language group has published its model, testing is not due to begin before 1982. The only satisfactory explanation is that the DES sees the APU as having reached the limit of its usefulness, and has no desire to throw good money after bad. Tests in English, mathematics, science and perhaps French are evidently more than enough to satisfy the legislature: looking at further areas of the curriculum may only uncover the kind of weakness which would require DES expenditure in order to sustain a concern for standards. There is, in any case, a risk of this with the science and mathematics tests, where the shortage of specialist teachers is of growing concern. For the executive to encourage researchers to peer underneath other stones would certainly be a work of supererogation. Monitoring is, after all, a contentious business, and what might have seemed a relatively simple task in the heady days of the six lines of development looks more and more like a set of indefensible assumptions. For the civil servants, as for the politicians in both parties, the APU may have served its purpose. The extension even to a foreign language will be at age thirteen only, and the testing in English, mathematics and science could easily become a three or four year cycle rather than an annual event. It is true, too, that testing of any kind other than simple paper and pencil multichoice tests gets enormously expensive. The academics and HMI who made a virtue of performance testing promised far more than it could ever deliver: DES officials caught up in endless meetings on the Rasch model and item banking must now be aware of this, and the political problems of schools have shifted from back-to-basics to falling rolls, parental choice and local authority cuts. The obvious course is to let the APU wither on the vine.

This may seem to do less than justice to the commitment of DES officials to educational inquiry for its own sake. But an inquiry into the civil service has pointed out that the talent which turns bureaucrats into mandarins is that of resolving issues by 'a cynical balancing act, devoid of moral content' (Kellner and Crowther-Hunt, 1980). The well-meaning (if misguided) faith in the educational virtues of national monitoring held by some teachers, academics, administrators and inspectors may appeal to HMI, but will cut no ice with career civil servants. Their concern is to do what is necessary with as little trouble as possible: hence the secrecy in which the APU was set up, the humbug which has cloaked its real purpose, and the discreet limitation of the scale of the operation once the failure of the new nostrum has become manifest. This is the most likely explanation of the takeover of the unit by the civil servants in June 1979. The HMI who had taken over the unit from Kay — Tom Marjoram — stayed little over two years. Soon after delivering his encomium to its merits, Marjoram was moved to the Midlands and the key job of administrative head went to a civil servant in the DES. Only professional aspects of the APU work remain the responsibility of an HMI. And by disposing of the coordinating group in early 1980, the process of severing the unit from its brave beginnings has been taken a step further.

And nothing is said now about the connection between the APU and the Educational Disadvantage Unit of which it was originally a minor part. The matrix sampling approach of the APU cannot, by definition, identify poorly performing schools or pupils; and in any case, what level of performance defines disadvantage? Despite the huge sums of money spent on test development, the APU language unit had to admit that it could do no better than the 1950 Ministry of Education definition of literacy as the ability 'to read and write for the practical purposes of daily life'. Sadly, the researchers observed that 'we still lack the means to measure how well even that apparently simple criterion is being fulfilled'. So although 'under-achievement' remains in the APU's terms of reference as a reminder of its devious beginnings, the questions which it raises are still unanswered:

> Is there some agreed-upon level of performance in any of the areas under test against which underachievement can be measured? If there is I have not been able to discover it ... It is yet to be made clear whether underachievement is to be related to an individual's capacity or to some specified competency level or simply to some norm-referenced level of performance as the standard. (Brown, 1980)

The APU, indeed, seems quite uninterested in tackling these questions. Two members of the APU science development team (Professor Black and Dr Harlen) have embarked on a research project to investigate 'standard' performance levels in relation to science testing, but they have been funded by the Social Sciences Research Council (SSRC), and not by the DES.

It is an interesting irony, though, that an attempt by the APU to test the educational performance of West Indian children, on the grounds that 'if significant deficiencies in performance are identified a serious attempt will be made to do something about it', has come in for serious criticism from a variety of bodies. The quotation comes from an APU report sent to representatives of the West Indian community, teachers and local authorities. A press report (*The Times Educational Supplement*, 9 January 1981) states that the plan has been criticised by the APU's statistics advisory group: 'A much broader sample was required to give an unbiased picture ... the plan to compare the performance of West Indian with indigenous children in the same school was statistically unsound'. The plan is evidently an attempt by the APU to justify itself by furnishing this evidence for the Rampton committee set up by the DES to study the education of ethnic minorities. But CON has urged extreme caution with these tests, recommending neither acceptance nor rejection. Subsequently, organisations representing the West Indian community and teachers' own organisation have voiced strong opposition on the grounds that the tests will provoke hostility from parents and pupils and risk the misuse of the results by those anxious to make a racist point. The fact that the APU is prepared to advocate testing in such a controversial area suggests either a remarkable insensitivity to public concerns, or a desperate attempt to revive the fading fortunes of the unit inside the DES. In the event, the attempt failed. For in May 1981, the Secretary of State (Mr Carlisle) announced in Parliament that plans for this APU survey had been dropped. According to a report in *The Times Educational Supplement* (8 May 1981), the DES 'has accepted criticisms that the APU survey would have done little more than confirm what was already known without indicating causes or likely remedies'. This is further evidence of the APU's weakened power base within the DES, and of growing scepticism about the real value of the APU's elaborate and costly testing apparatus.

Finally, mention must be made of a confidential report made by the statistics advisory group of the APU which, according to *The Times Educational Supplement*, accepts the criticisms made of the Rasch model and casts doubt on the entire basis of APU year-by year comparisons. The report maintains that:

> The theoretical and technical objections to the model had not been answered; another independent statistical authority should be asked for a view; it should be made clear in any APU reports that comparisons based on the model were purely experimental.

This last point is particularly serious, since it casts doubt on the weight to be attached to any comparative analysis — such as will appear in the 1981 report of the second year's mathematics testing — and on the value to LEAs of the NFER's APU-linked testing described in the next chapter.

It may be, then, that during the 1980s the APU will adopt a low profile as the ineffectiveness of national monitoring becomes more evident. But no one should assume for a moment that if and when the APU declines, the influence of the APU's work on schools and teachers will decline. For the APU's terms of reference include the commitment 'To promote the conduct of assessment in cooperation with local education authorities and teachers', and it is clear from events across the Atlantic that the real threat to the curriculum from attempts to evaluate it comes not from random sampling at national level, but from blanket testing and curriculum interventions at local level. And also, since any form of testing is reductionist in nature, there is the danger that as APU-inspired tests penetrate LEAs and schools, so will the scope of curriculum experience be diminished. In the next chapter, the other — and potentially much more serious — threat resulting from the APU's activities will be examined: the threat to the breadth and quality of the school curriculum which stems not from national monitoring, but from the use of APU tests at local level.

NOTES

1 **The Black Papers.** Towards the end of the 1960s progressive education became a contentious issue. The publication of *Fight for Education* in 1969 marked the first of a series of similar 'Black Papers', each containing a number of articles of variable quality, broadly critical of progressive ideas in education from university to primary school.

2 **DES.** The Department of Education and Science is the department of national government responsible for education policy which replaced the Ministry of Education in 1963. Its head is the Secretary of State, and it is responsible for schools, further education and higher education. Its officials are permanent civil servants and, as such, must be parties to the Official Secrets Act. It is responsible for ensuring that its policies are implemented by local education authorities. Her Majesty's Inspectorate is a body of inspectors (HMIs) attached to the DES, but separately responsible to the Secretary for State. They are also civil servants. Their role was defined in 1840 as one of assistance rather than control, and was muted during the 1960s. Since the mid-seventies their opinions have been more in evidence.

3 **Yellow Book.** During 1975 the DES was asked — on the initiative of the then Prime Minister, Mr Callaghan — to produce a confidential report on standards in education in schools. The four areas investigated were: teaching of basics in primary schools; the curriculum in comprehensives; public examinations; and 16-19 education. The report remains secret, but it was leaked to the press shortly before Mr Callaghan's 1976 speech at Ruskin College, Oxford. The report is known as the Yellow Book, and its criticisms are generally intemperate. But it served as the basis for the Ruskin speech, and for the agenda of the subsequent 'debates'. Its influence is evident in the 1977 Green Paper. On the APU, it states that the unit 'was set up as recently as August 1974 ... In terms of the curriculum the priorities are to follow up the recommendations of the Bullock Report ... to evaluate and pursue the reports on testing mathematical aptitude (TAMS) ... and to make a start in considering the assessment of science'. (Lawton, 1980).

4 School Evaluation and Local Education Authorities

Belief in the power of testing reflects a particular view of school and society, and therefore owes much to instinctive feelings and the tides of fashion. By 1977 these were lapping around local authority committee rooms up and down the country, and the result was considerable pressure on officers to monitor the school curriculum by means of quantitative instruments.

The pressure could come from any of three directions. First, there was party political pressure stemming from sloganising about standards in education. Thus, in the autumn of 1977, the Conservative Party asked its research department to make 'a full-scale study on how standards in education can be most effectively monitored ... There appears to have been a re-awakening of interest in monitoring schoolchildren's standards of achievement, and several authorities are examining possible testing schemes' (*The Times*, 2 November 1977). There are still a few — very few — local authorities where decisions on education do not split along party lines, despite clear majorities: but in the main, the politicising of local government has been one of the remorseless trends of the 1970s and one which owes much to the 1974 reorganisation of local government by the Health administration. This is now widely recognised as an appalling miscalculation, but its dire effects on the administration of education are less widely known. The main cause is the unwieldy and discredited concept of corporate management, which has exposed educational decisions to corporate control and therefore to political influence. The professional judgment of education officers must give way to the hardline view of the ruling party caucus, and in the late seventies there appeared to be a lot of votes in the notion of school monitoring. It attracts support from all parties, but in the UK, as in the USA, right-wingers find it particularly appealing. These politicians often have backgrounds in industry or commerce, where quantitative methods are associated with profits figures and with management techniques. Increasing expenditure on schools makes education an obvious target, along with the gut feeling that schools are soft-centred William Tyndales,[1] purveying wet left-wing attitudes at the expense of rigour and rugged competition.

The evidence, though, shows that schools and teachers are not like this at all. Just before the 1979 election, *The Times Educational Supplement* conducted a poll which showed that the majority of schoolteachers would vote Conservative, particularly in primary schools: only as one moved to higher education and the universities did a Labour majority appear. And in 1978, the HMI national primary survey showed that most teachers were using didactic rather than discovery methods and were preoccupied with the basic skills of literacy and numeracy, to the point of saturation: 'The teaching of skills in isolation, whether in language or mathematics, does not produce the best results' (*Primary Education in England*, DES, 1978). The national secondary survey, published a year later, confirmed the picture. The curriculum of the 1902 grammar school had, it seemed, almost all the secondary schools in the land in its clammy grip. 'In recent years the pressure of external examinations has affected more and more pupils': teaching methods were mainly traditional, and differentiation by ability (and by sex) was the rule. Both surveys show school systems dominated by attitudes which an emphasis on teaching the basics could only reinforce. Both surveys provoked the HMI into calling for a broader curriculum, less constrained by external pressures of a fashionable but counter-educational nature.

A second influence on local authority attitudes to monitoring is the example of APU monitoring at national level. This has given an aura of respectability to testing which has appealed, perhaps, as much to administrators as politicians: 'Clean limbed go-getting CEOs (Chief Education Officers) with their noses to the wind and eyes to the main chance are eagerly assisting the DES and the APU in their efforts to drag us kicking and screaming into the nineteenth century' (Stones, 1979).

Third, there is the expressed APU intention to make its own instruments available at local level by means of the NFER item bank. This is the third task in its terms of reference — 'To promote the conduct of assessments in cooperation with the local education authorities and teachers' — and the 1977 Green Paper declared that in testing, 'greater consistency of practice can only be beneficial'. The DES has been anxious to promote sample testing rather than blanket testing, but in many LEAs the sheer momentum for extensive testing has proved irresistible. In a speech in early 1977, the head of the APU (Brian Kay, HMI) had to say that 'we must guard against the danger of over-testing. After all, learning is the main object', and by the end of the year his successor (Tom Marjoram, HMI) was even more explicit: 'Blanket testing by an outside agent is wasteful, inefficient, expensive, and possibly unsusceptible to comparison with APU outcomes'. At the same conference, the director of the NFER (Alfred Yates) said that 'the purposes of monitoring can be served by testing only a sample of the children in each school', and the Secretary of State (Mrs Williams) urged LEAs not to jump the gun with blanket testing, and to 'keep in step' with the APU (1977 annual general meeting of the NFER).

Testing — the Inexorable Force

These calls for restraint were necessary, but unrealistic. For to many serving on education committees the DES message appeared to be that testing was good. So how could it be bad? This inconsistency was spotted by the Conservative MP (later a government minister) Timothy Raison, who is thought to represent more liberal opinion in his party. He noted that the Green Paper argued against blanket tests 'pitched at a single level' which could be 'irrelevant for some and beyond the reach of others', and asked:

> If pitching tests at a certain level is irrelevant for some and beyond the reach of others when it comes to blanket testing, how can it be acceptable for sample testing, of which the APU and the Secretary of State approve? And is coaching for the attainment of minimum levels of literacy and numeracy really such a bad thing? (*The Times*, 14 November 1978)

Raison went on to argue against blanket testing for the purposes of school accountability, or as a selection tool, but for it as a diagnostic device — by analogy with school medical inspection: 'it would be used to direct resources and special attention where the need for them becomes apparent'.

The logic of Raison's argument seems to me to be superior to that of the DES and the APU: if the tests are as good as the APU wishes us to think, this seems a sound enough case for MCT despite the horrors of the American experience. But the premise is unsound: we have no way of determining educational health, in the way in which a doctor can determine medical health. For one thing, there is substantial agreement on what we mean by a healthy person, while few can agree on the attributes of an educated person. And for another, we can determine medical health without influencing the pupil's normal conduct, regimen or life-style. Looking down his throat or measuring his blood pressure do not disturb the process of breathing — but all are agreed that these are adequate tests for establishing certain aspects of health. Neither is true of educational tests: we are not sure what they measure, and we know that they impose a preordinate view of what we are trying to measure on the process we are measuring. It is also the case that the act of testing influences the learning process: 'The Unit is well aware that it is not possible to carry out tests of performance without affecting current practice in the schools' (DES *Report on Education*, 'Assessing the Performance of Pupils', No. 93, 1978).

There is, in short, a fundamental inconsistency about the APU's approach to local testing. The same DES report states that 'The APU task is to assess what is happening, not to change it'. But an APU document 'The Unit's Approach' of March 1977 refers to local monitoring as 'a form of quality control'. This implies that the purpose of monitoring is to detect blemishes in the product, and do something about them. Little wonder, therefore, that the bland 'aerial photography' approach to testing in the APU's various public documents seems too subtle by half in the council chambers.

In practice, a variety of reasons can be given for justifying monitoring by LEAs, once the decision has been taken to do it. For a cautious view, here is that of an HMI working for the APU: 'Local education authorities need knowledge of what is happening in their schools to help them identify priorities' (Peaker, 1979). This is said in the context of special education, and the DES has gone out of its way to stress that although the Warnock Report (1978) called for the monitoring of whole age groups to identify children with special educational needs, 'such monitoring would not necessarily involve testing' (*Report on Education*, No. 93).

Another argument has been put forward by a chief education officer (and member of CON):

> The more I know about testing the more I am opposed to the idea of a simplistic test given to all children ... The monitoring and continous assessment of pupils' progress is quite another matter. Testing materials carefully selected and intelligently applied can be an aid and an objective check to teachers which can help to complete their profiles of pupils ... (Boulter, 1978).

Testing is, on this argument, not so much for the benefit of LEAs and the ordering of their 'priorities' but rather a tool to help teachers in schools. Here, 'objective' means, presumably, 'using national norms': after all, every teacher makes use of formal and informal criterion-referenced tests to make sure pupils understand the work in hand. Setting aside the difficulty of giving much meaning to the notion of an 'objective' test, we might ask why teachers' own tests are not themselves sufficient? The DES answer is: 'A class or even a school can be an isolated community and it is sometimes useful for such a group to have the opportunity to measure up against the world beyond '(*Report on Education,* No. 93).

I find this an unconvincing argument. In mathematics, a teacher would have to be remarkably insensitive not to notice the relation between a child's work and his professional understanding of competence and excellence: a primary head teacher would be professionally inadequate not to be aware of such shortcomings on his staff. To talk about the need to 'measure up against the world beyond' when we seem to be talking about professional standards is cant, and unhelpful cant at that. The remedy is not a national test but a programme of in-service training. In language, Stibbs (1979) has listed a number of ways in which teachers 'can replace the apparatus of testing'. For example, a teacher can note how often the child asks for spellings, and thus diagnose misunderstandings; can note the clarity of his speech, his ability to explain or to convey a message, and so on:

> Such evidence is too often ignored in favour of more standardised infomation which, though it may appear to dignify and quantify the assessment of children's language, really confuses it. Just to look at a page of a child's writing alongside one from a year before is a better indicator of progress than a test result or some quasi-objective measure of improvement.

It seems extraordinary that the Bullock Committee, while far from insensitive to the work of language teachers in the classroom, could fail to see that their unqualified enthusiasm for national monitoring would be inimical to the causes they sought to further.

The Response of the Local Education Authorities

It is not easy to establish the extent of local authority involvement in language and mathematics testing. When Mrs Renee Short MP asked a Parliamentary question on the subject, the Secretary of State's reply was unhelpful:

The Department does not collect information from local authorities about test schemes in use in their areas. A number of LEAs conduct tests for their own purposes, but the Department has no regular arrangements for collecting systematic information about them (Hansard, 11 March 1980).

It may be the case that such information is not collected on a regular basis, but an unpublished survey was prepared for the APU in 1979 — presumably by HMI, who have close links with LEAs and, as part of their job, inform the DES on what is happening.

The APU survey obtained information about 92 of the 104 LEAs in England and Wales. Of these, 68 had a testing programme; 11 were discussing one; and 59 were testing all pupils (not just a sample) in the age bracket chosen. Seven was the most popular age for testing, followed by age ten or eleven. Thus there were 134 instances of testing during the primary years (five to eleven), but only 22 of testing post eleven. Most LEAs were testing pupils at only one age bracket, but 13 were testing pupils no less than three times during compulsory education. Reading was much the most popular area tested: 58 authorities were using reading tests, and 27 mathematics tests. Tests of English including spelling and literacy were used by 15, and another 19 used intelligence tests of some kind. Only one was testing for science, but two were testing emotional stability.

During 1979 I sent a simple questionnaire to each of the 96 LEAs in England, and obtained 45 replies. There were only four questions:

1 What steps has your authority taken, at the time of writing, to introduce performance testing in the authority's secondary schools?

2 In what ways, if any, is it the intention that the results of these local tests should be linked with the national tests carried out by the DES Assessment of Performance Unit?

3 In what ways, if any, is it envisaged that the tests may be used so as to lead to curriculum change in schools?

4 If it is *not* the authority's intention to introduce monitoring schemes for school performance — or if such schemes have been dropped after prior experiment — please indicate the reasons that have prevailed for taking this course of action.

Of the 45 authorities responding, 17 had testing programmes of some kind, and of these 13 were carrying out blanket testing at some age or other. That left 28 authorities with no testing programme at present, although 9 of these had the matter under consideration. The unpublished APU survey showed that 24 authorities had no programme but 11 were discussing one. The dividing line is by no means clear cut, since some of the monitoring authorities appear reluctant to acknowledge this. One, for example, has offered a nil return to the first three questions, but in reply to (4) written: 'We have developed maths and English/literacy Record Cards in the past three years which act as a form of monitoring'. Another supplies the Richmond Tests of Basic Skills to all schools, 'to enable them to use them for all pupils aged eight to thirteen each year. Almost all schools take advantage of this facility', and since the scores are entered on profile sheets and transfer cards, this is in effect a testing programme in all but name. It is worth noting that the Richmond Tests are based on the American IOWA tests of basic skills, and are published in the UK with the offer of a computer marking facility. 'The test is advertised as a diagnostic instrument but many local authorities use it as a norm-reference test for making comparisons between pupils and schools' (Galton, 1979). A third authority 'has no policy for the regular administration of tests at secondary level', but the Wide Span Reading Test 'has been administered to secondary pupils on two recent occasions'. Another authority states that 'All secondary schools will now be expected to give the Nelson Cognitive Abilities Tests (the Richmond tests) [sic] to pupils in their third year', and collects a ten per cent sample of the results: 'though this is of value in monitoring standards, it does not allow us to identify particular schools'. But some authorities have no inhibitions of this kind: 'Results do identify individual schools and are followed up'; 'Schools which appear to be experiencing difficulties or which are doing exceptionally well are followed up by visits from advisers/officers/psychologists'; 'One of the objectives ... is the identification of schools needing special help'; 'the results for individual schools provide useful information for the County Advisory Staff'.

It is certainly clear that of the 51 authorities which did not respond to my inquiry, virtually all must have committed themselves to testing programmes. For the APU survey found 68 had programmes, and my inquiry disclosed only 17. The fact that 51 and 17 make 68 may not be significant. The failure of the 51 authorities to reply may be due to pressure of work or a certain coyness about the scale of their monitoring operations. My own questionnaire (which was directed at secondary age testing) showed that all the testing authorities monitored reading performance, mainly at ages 12, 13 and 14 and using a variety of tests (Richmond, Edinburgh, Gap/Gapadol, NFER EH 1). Most tested at the same ages in mathematics, mainly using the NFER EF or FG tests. The choice of testing age will take into account the age of transfer between schools in the authority, and at least one authority uses test results to facilitate the differentiation of pupils upon transfer:

> All fourth year students in middle schools (age range 12–13) are given three tests in arithmetic in the Spring and this information is used to help classify children on transfer to high schools. The top thirty per cent are given a further test to select the more able children in mathematics.

A great many authorities indicated that they were watching closely the possibility of linking their own tests with those of the APU by means of the NFER LEASIB project, and seven appeared to have taken the idea a step further:

> If tests are introduced in the future we would link them with the National Tests carried out by the DES Assessment of Performance Unit.

> Discussions are taking place with the APU (Mathematics) at the NFER concerning the possibility of using their Item Bank in the Mathematics Screening which is carried out at the top end of every Primary School each year.

> This group is exploring the potential of item banking with a view to anticipating the availability of the LEASIB facility currently being developed by the NFER.

> ... Such a link could not be ruled out in the future.

> If proper conclusions can be drawn linking the results with APU tests this will be done but it is not a primary intention of testing.

> Hopefully (local and national tests will be linked) through the LEASIB project.

> Hopefully, the APU will provide assessment materials which will provide a basis for this comparison.

Most of the respondents showed an awareness of the link between testing and curriculum change, which question (3) was intended to disclose. The usual response here was to refer to the role of LEA advisers: 'Results from schools are returned to the Education Division and monitored. Follow-up may occur or provide basis for discussion with Education Advisers'. In another authority, 'all the screening and survey procedures ... are dealt with by the educational psychologists', and as a result of blanket tests at seven, eleven and seventeen in reading , 'meetings of heads and staffs of schools with difficulty are held. Action results in more interest being shown in the teaching of reading. Secondary schools have begun to be aware of the need for. curriculum change'. Using educational psychologists to administer reading tests in order to change the secondary curriculum seems a quite bizarre procedure. Another reply referred to the use of tests to identify 'deficiencies in basic skills'. There was often a reference to the use of resources: 'Follow-up action takes the form of allocation of additional resources where this is possible'. In another reply to question (3), there was an interesting emphasis: 'Not *change* in schools curricula — reinforcement of County Core almost inevitable'.

This authority was administering mathematics tests at ages seven, eleven and fourteen. On further inquiry, I was told:

> The tests we use are designed to be valid in relation to our County Core Curriculum, thus it is known in the County that core topics only are being tested and some teachers will give extra attention to the core items and 'inevitably' reinforce the core. The core was produced after massive consulation with every teacher in the County concerned with mathematics and also with people from industry and commerce.

The use of tests to define 'guidelines' or a 'core' will be discussed in the next section. In general, the questionnaire replies show that LEAs are aware that testing will have a backwash effect, but are either loath to admit it or would prefer to think that its effects will be desirable. As one authority put it: 'You may wish to know that we do not *intend* to change the curriculum by this process, but there will certainly be changes as by-products'. This kind of double-think has, of course, characterised the APU's approach to the matter and it is hardly surprising that LEAs find themselves in similar difficulties.

Before looking more closely at the effects of LEA monitoring, it is worth looking at some points from the responses of LEAs not committed to testing procedures. It is an interesting reflection on LEA attitudes to testing that (assuming the APU survey is reliable) virtually all the non-testing authorities were glad to complete my questionnaires and indicate this, while all those not replying to my specific questions on testing appear to be committed to monitoring of some kind. One reply illustrates the bipartisan nature of much LEA policy making, and brings out vividly the political basis of decisions on school monitoring:

> A working group was set up to advise the appropriate committee on ways that could be adopted to assess pupil performance. The working group met over a period of two years and then made its recommendations. The committee members bridled at the technical language of the report — and there the matter rests ... The working group's proposals advocated the development of a 'checklist' of basic skills for use by teachers in natural classroom settings. Emphasis would thus have been placed on the acquisition of basic skills. The committee to which

we reported in June of this year had no memory, as it were (of these proposals). Its composition had changed radically from that which advocated the setting up of the working group. Moreover, Mr Callaghan's Ruskin speech, the Green Paper etc. were things of the past.

In two other authorities, the issue of monitoring has remained a matter for the officers:

> The Director of Education feels that it is better to leave it to the APU to achieve some sort of national experience of widescale monitoring, and not to intervene with LEA initiatives at present.

> Although I have not put this matter before Committee, I would feel that such testing is valuable only if (a) its purposes are clear, and (b) it is of ultimate value to the schools and, more particularly, to individual pupils.

Four other authorities see monitoring as inappropriate or even alien to their accepted ways of running an education service:

> The matter has not been discussed at a formal level, and there has been no pressure either in Committee or among officers for the introduction of a structured testing system.

> Monitoring of performance through public examination results and curriculum change through curriculum returns are aspects of the Authority's present activities. They are quite difficult enough!

> This authority ... has always given its schools considerable authority and freedom.

> The authority supports strongly the autonomy of head teachers ... it is at the entire discretion of a head teacher whether — and how — he organises testing in his own school.

Lastly, there is the case of an authority which had been involved, since 1976, in re-examining the curriculum in seven pilot schools in conjunction with HMI and arising from the document *Curriculum 11-16*:

> We would depart from the underlying implications of your questionnaire over the word 'testing', not as a matter of philosophy necessarily but simply because that is not the way we have so far approached the problem ... Having analysed their curriculum in some considerable depth our seven pilot schools are now considering how to assess the effectiveness of their work in the subject disciplines.

In short, as a result of studying the curriculum, matters of assessment may now be tackled: assessment comes not before consideration of the curriculum, but after it.

A Closer Look at Local Authority Testing

The case for LEA monitoring of school performance in order to improve the work of schools has been made by the chief education officer for Somerset (Taylor, 1979). Blanket testing of eight year olds
for reading began in this authority in 1974: since 1979, Edinburgh
Reading Tests have been administered on a blanket basis at ages
seven, eleven and thirteen. Teachers do most of the marking; schools
get 'a breakdown of results and a county norm'. In mathematics, the
NFER item bank was used to test primary school leavers in a 1979
pilot project: 'All being well, I hope this single test will become
county-wide, providing each school with its mean score, the county
mean and the standard deviation. It will be standardised with the
APU question bank'. Taylor's article describes two further developments in 'the integration of assessment with curriculum'. First, in
language, a group of advisers devised 'a checklist of skills in reading,
writing and spoken language' for consideration by a group of primary
and secondary teachers. The guidelines do not seem to be linked to
any specific tests, but rather with specific behavioural objectives.
The article gives an example from the spelling block: 'Does the child
display an understanding of the following spelling conventions in his
own written composition? (1) Letters which can be put together/word
families? (2) Letter/sound relationships? (3) Sequence of vowels and
consonants? (4) Adding prefixes and suffixes? ...' The intention here
is that the objectives should be used to assess the effectiveness of the
teacher's work:

> Thus we are trying to move to more effective diagnostic teaching in
> the spirit of Marjoram ... who said 'every individual pupil's perfor-
> mance certainly needs to be known — but at the school level where
> strengths can be encouraged and weaknesses remedied on the spot'.

This aspect of APU philosophy has, secondly, been applied to the
area of mathematics, and the authority's *Mathematics Guidelines* are
published commercially. The results of these checklists form, with
the reading test results, the pupil record card which is also a transfer
card. A formalised checklist has also been produced for use in infant
schools on first-year children 'whom observation suggests may be at
risk ... There is no doubt that much earlier referrals have been
facilitated'. With regard to all these developments, Taylor notes two
aspects: 'One is fact, the second assertion':

> First, there has been a very high level of teacher acceptance and en-
> thusiasm; and secondly, the quality of learning, particularly perhaps in

our smaller schools, and the sensitivity of teachers to individual pupils' strengths and weaknesses is already markedly enhanced.

On the first aspect, there can be no doubt that what has enabled LEAs to institute testing programmes — even blanket testing as in this case — has been the eager cooperation of the teachers and, at primary level at any rate, head teachers. It seems clear that any group of teachers brought together under the aegis of the LEA can be relied upon to produce at least a 'checklist' of basic skills, and may well be prepared to go much further: 'Primary and middle school staffs have been virtually unanimous in supporting uniform standardised tests and say they have found previous results useful in influencing their classroom work' (Taylor, 1979). Furthermore, teachers wrote strongly supporting the Somerset testing programme 'in spite of the expressed opposition of their professional association, the only one to adopt this stance'.

This is a reference to the National Union of Teachers, which draws the bulk of its membership from primary schools (and with which I have had no connection). The NUT lays great stress on the autonomy of the individual teacher, and any head who has been involved in curriculum innovation knows how valuable an asset this quality can be. At the same time, schools need an agreed understanding of what their educational policy should be, and it seems important to resolve questions of this kind at LEA and national level at a time when there is no agreed political consensus on what education should be about. My own view is that, in its influence on Schools Council curriculum policies, the NUT has been misguided in a rigid interpretation of teacher autonomy in subject terms and in resisting attempts to shape whole curriculum policies. And in this respect it has certainly been out of step with the views of its more thoughtful members in secondary schools.

With regard to LEA monitoring, however, I think the NUT officials have correctly recognised from the start that this development might seriously damage the quality of the education offered by individual teachers. In their perceptions of American schemes, in their analysis of APU policy and in condemning LEA blanket testing, the NUT seems to me to have shown a shrewd and far-sighted grasp of the political issues involved and the educational issues at stake. Its CON representatives on the APU were surely right to oppose from the beginning the suggestion that the entire range of experiences offered to pupils in a schools curriculum should be made the subject of quantitative measurement; and ultimately, of course, the LEA representatives (for reasons which we cannot fathom) came to adopt this view in voting against a continuance of work by the PSD group. In their opposition to blanket LEA testing, the NUT had the support of the APU, the Secretary of State (Mrs Williams), and the director of the NFER. The NUT's document *Guidance to Divisions on Local Authority Testing* (E.55, 1977) is a succinct summary of the ways in which testing might be justified, and used the reservations of the Bullock Report to good effect in drawing attention to its dangers:

> The Union agrees that early detection of learning difficulties is vital but is disturbed that such heavy reliance is placed on standardised tests ... The Bullock Committee does not favour the use of standardised tests alone as they can only present narrow measures of ability ... Single-value measures of progress are not only unhelpful to the teaching profession, but encourage an over-simplification of the situation when results are represented to a wider audience.

The NUT is also right to argue that areas of need exposed by testing will not necessarily receive extra resources, and that shunting inadequate resources around from one area to another 'would be unacceptable because it would benefit some schools and children at the expense of others'. One authority which operates blanket reading tests of seven year olds has withdrawn peripatetic remedial help. Heads are therefore teaching much more so that class teachers can withdraw small groups for special help. There is thus less time for the whole curriculum planning which the HMI national primary survey identified as a major priority in school leadership.

The readiness with which teachers have given their time and support to LEA monitoring and guidelining operations, despite union advice, reflects not so much naivety as a helpful willingness to cooperate with LEAs, a responsiveness to the national mood of the time, and a desire for a supportive framework which, at first sight, appears to make a difficult job a bit easier. But standardised test results and behavioural guidelines are a dubious crutch, even for bad teachers: for good teachers they are at best another administrative inconvenience, at worst a constraint on a teacher's imagination — his most priceless gift. Taylor (1979) reports that in Somerset each year the reading-test norms 'have been higher than the previous year', and quotes an adviser with approval: 'children do not grow taller by being measured but they are more likely to stand up straight'. On the contrary: basic competency tests in one or two subjects simply guarantee that teachers will tend to stress these subjects, and so distort the curriculum — children are more likely to grow up stunted. Taylor is at pains to state his awareness of the dangers of testing.

His main argument for testing is essentially a managerial one: 'Teachers and other professionals had all too frequently no systematic check on their pupils' progress and similarly we simply did not know year by year whether overall standards in the key curriculum areas were rising or falling'. Yet he justifies testing by pointing to the fact that 'assessment, and testing in one form or another, is an integral, indeed unavoidable, ingredient of all effective teaching'. So although teachers have always assessed, they have also lacked 'systematic check'. It is by no means clear, though, that the second aspect of Somerset's testing programme mentioned by Taylor — his assertion that the quality of learning has been enhanced — is the result of teachers scrutinising the checklists in English and mathematics, or of the in-service training courses which were arranged, we are told, as a fundamental part of the guidelines operation. And any evaluation of a new initiative of this kind must allow for the Hawthorne, halo and Matthew effects[2].

As for the argument that only testing can provide information on standards, this would seem to overlook the existence of several readily available measures, and most obviously public examinations at sixteen plus. How the results of commercial reading tests can significantly enhance those professionally conducted examinations like O-level and CSE must be a puzzle to many teachers. It is indeed, difficult to see how the altogether more elaborate APU tests can provide more information. Kay (1975) argues that the APU data were needed because, first, forty-five per cent of pupils do not receive a graded O-level/CSE pass, and are therefore not examined; and, second, it was 'common prudence' not to wait eleven years before checking on the educational process. But neither argument stands up. The APU results only show that a certain proportion of pupils appear to know certain things — the ignorance of the rest is simply confirmed; and — as the Americans have found — NAEP/APU data are of negligible value either to teachers or administrators.

The most ominous aspect of LEA testing is any attempt to link testing with curriculum change, and Somerset is not alone in coupling an emphasis on monitoring with the production of lists of guidelines or core elements. In language, these can readily be justified by reference to the Bullock Report; teachers can be reassured that the aim is to help screen, rather than monitor. The weasel words here are 'objective' and 'diagnostic'. Even if an objective test existed, its use and interpretation would be subjective; and any diagnostic or criterion-referenced test can be used to provide standardised norms. The trouble with guidelines and core statements is that either they are so vague as to be virtually meaningless, or so detailed as to be either unmanageable or a constraint on the learning process. They are in essence an impoverished substitute for a proper educational policy for the whole curriculum of a school. Once that policy is clear, its resolution into curriculum areas can be extended as formally as the staff concerned think necessary. But to start with subject-bound lists of concepts and objectives is to imperil curriculum planning and reduce the learning experience to what can be written down and — perhaps — what can be tested. Minimum cores quickly become — for poor teachers — the maximum experience. Their effect is not to enhance but to diminish. Hence the connection with monitoring; even if the guidelines are not themselves monitored, the fact of monitoring makes reductionism respectable. So it is that teachers who, a few years before, were rejoicing in their freedom from an examination at eleven plus can be found in committee rooms and teachers' centres happily forging new curriculum shackles for their classrooms and, alas, their pupils. Teachers are deskilling themselves by taking part in such exercises, since the aim is to impose teacher-proof areas of content on to schools, rather than help schools solve their own curriculum problems within a supportive and professional framework. As a primary head in one authority remarked to me: 'The maths guidelines really reflect the views of the adviser, who is keen on the Fletcher books. Schools are not yet required to conform, but there is pressure.'

In addition to the results of public examinations, LEAs can get a good idea of their overall performance by noting the proportion of pupils passing into higher education and the proportion staying on for post-sixteen education: these are both comparable with national data. From year to year they can compare attendance levels and the number of pupils suspended from schools or diverted into special units. On a non-numerical basis they can record the participation of LEA teachers on national schemes, and their awards or publications, and the success of their pupils at such ventures as youth orchestras and Duke of Edinburgh Awards. But in uncertain times people clutch at the promise of hard data, and in many authorities initial flirtations with reading tests are leading to calls for an extension to mathematics and a link with the APU by means of the NFER project. Before looking at this in more detail, it is worth recording the comments of the participants in an LEA already undertaking blanket reading tests, and contemplating a similar move in mathematics as the result of sample surveys.

The first comment came from the deputy head of a 13-18 school fed by several middle schools. The effect of mathematics testing in these schools was already being felt in the secondary school: 'the maths tests are very restricting on the pupils' curriculum experience in mathematics, and in science too'. The next came from an adviser for the authority with special responsibility for remedial education, and therefore first-hand knowledge of the reading tests of seven years olds designed primarily as a screening device:

> We give the reading test across the board to all pupils. The schools administer and mark the test, and complete the record sheet. This goes to the county remedial staff and pupils with a VRQ [Verbal Reasoning Quotient] less than 85 are seen again. As far as I'm concerned its purpose is entirely diagnostic, and we use it to allocate additional staff to weak schools. The test is not very sensitive at the top end of the scale. I think schools have appreciated this opportunity to appraise their own situation, and so far there has been a slight improvement each year for three years. It's true, though, that it has concentrated the attention of schools only on the teaching of reading, and we've also devoted a lot of in-service training to it. Now there are moves to extend the scheme, but the language assessment panel at county hall finds it difficult to agree. I feel any extension of county testing might break the goodwill we have in schools. Further screening at eleven plus would not be popular in schools, but the LEA might be pushing for testing because it is a fashionable idea. The true cost of testing has at present been concealed by teacher goodwill.

In reply to my specific questions about the effects of testing, this adviser made the following points:

> Many heads objected to the blanket testing at seven-plus on the grounds that they were also using their own, more extensive tests. Yes, it does happen that heads will say their school gets good results on the LEA tests not because their children are especially bright, but because their staff work harder. Then it seems unfair that other schools with poorer results but the same sort of children get extra help. To ensure fairness, pupils would have to be tested for IQ, to see which schools are making the most of their entry. Where do you stop? It could also be the case that an infant school head, by bothering less about reading, could get worse results and so secure extra staff. But the danger is more the reverse — that schools will pay too much attention to reading to get high scores, at the expense of other curriculum elements. The results of all this emphasis on testing are beginning to show in interviews for senior posts in schools. Governors and members like simple black and white statements, like test results. The possibility of linking up with national norms bothers me. As long as things are not too centrally dominated, it's all right. But this idea of the NFER of item

banking — it seems to me that if we're not careful, this can develop into a direct comparison between schools and between areas.

In another authority, I was able to interview a senior adviser who had
a direct involvement with the county's policy for testing and negotiations with the NFER on item banking. He talked frankly about the
difficulties raised by monitoring schemes:

> My experience with our work on monitoring reading shows a confu-
> sion of objectives. The educationists see the value of the tests as
> diagnostic. But the policitians say: what are the marks? The norms
> can't keep going up, year by year. What goes up must come down.
> That's going to be difficult, when it happens. As it is, they dislike the
> fact that fifty per cent of our pupils are below average! We do have
> some room for manoeuvre, though: we just have to play a political
> game. We want to improve education — the politicians have different
> objectives. There's certainly a danger that testing can go too far. Many
> primary schools are over-afflicted by reliance on the Schonell graded
> word list: heads see an improvement in results and think this is educa-
> tional progress. Emphasising testing doesn't help in this way. What-
> ever our promises, what the politicians remember are the figures. The
> first result of the primary maths test was that we were able to appoint
> some advisory teachers. But the members don't realise the full cost of a
> testing programme. We've misused our remedial teachers in making
> them do so much work on the blanket English testing. If we really
> moved into a rolling programme on maths, English, science and a
> foreign language, we'd need a special unit to do just that. It's by no
> means certain that the NFER LEASIB project can deliver the goods
> on maths and English. The maths may perhaps be all right. But no
> one could really accept the present scheme as a satisfactory test for
> language. Our secondary English advisers are very sceptical about it,
> and concerned about its narrowing effect on the curriculum. As for
> science, monitoring is almost irrelevant: basic curriculum planning
> and teaching technique are the real needs. Secondary teachers can't
> agree about whether there is a thing called science, rather than
> physics, chemistry and biology.

This authority had not yet made the step from LEA monitoring to
the production of guidelines. But I end this section with some comments of American teachers encumbered with the apparatus of
checklists, tests, recording results and defining cores (Denny, 1977):

> Filling out record sheets on each child is silly; I have to record that on
> March 30 Billy knows his facts from one to ten. So what! I'm going to
> check to see if he knows them anyway.

Administrators and counsellors say teachers in general do not for the most part utilise or know how to obtain information about their students from the standardised tests given. Teachers say the information is not useful. They say it does not aid in instruction because it tells them nothing they did not already know after two weeks of instruction and in no way implies how to remedy deficiencies that they already knew existed.

Curriculum guides are an old administrative siren song to which established teachers have long since learnt to cultivate a deaf ear.

The problem is they have gone over stuff. And over it. And over it. And never really know anything about it.

The Slough Connection: The APU/NFER Tie-up

Local authorities can easily drift into monitoring without considering exactly why. When so many other LEAs are buying tests, and when testing accords so naturally with the instincts of the controlling politicians, the educational aspects can get taken for granted. But eventually someone will need to ask the key questions. Are we testing schools, teachers or pupils? Do we seek an 'aerial view of performance', better ways of using resources, to establish what pupils have learnt, to differentiate pupils for transfer schemes, or to identify good and bad in the system — whether schools, teachers or pupils? Do we use our own tests, or commercial standardised tests? Who will do the testing, and at what cost? What will be the result of it all — will we make better decisions, improve the amount or the quality of what is learnt, change the nature of what is learnt, influence the attitudes of teachers in what ways? Exactly what are the tests actually testing, anyway?

The fact that most of these questions are unanswerable — behind the rhetoric of big science, testing is a matter of subjective judgement and guesswork — should not stop anyone asking them. Exposing the deep uncertainties about testing and its effects might allow common sense to seep in. Officers and members might then realise that there are other ways of establishing 'the health of the subject' (a polite way of talking about standards), or allocating resources, or deciding which schools need help. In the short run, testing might look cheaper than expanding an authority's professional support service to schools. In the long run, it could prove exceedingly damaging.

There are three critical decisions to be taken when an authority contemplates the slippery slope of monitoring performance. The first is the most difficult — do we or don't we? The questionnaire replies suggest that an authority which keeps clear of testing will have a strong tradition of localism, devolving power on to schools and heads; an education staff committed to this tradition rather than the bubble reputation of novelty or tough-minded centralism; and elected members with minds of their own and roots in the authority's established approach to an education service. The second decision is whether to use sample testing or blanket testing. As a rule, the only palpable result of testing English is to confirm the advisers' view of which schools need extra help. The APU has argued that a ten per cent sample will be sufficient for LEA testing, and none of the blanket-testing authorities has advanced evidence, as far as I know, to disprove this view.

The third decision is temptingly simple to take once testing has been established. Why not use tests which allow us to compare our performance with national norms? The members will then have the satisfaction of knowing that, despite a five per cent cut in education spending in the authority, the language norms are still one per cent above the national levels. And teachers can be assured that comparing their pupils' mathematics performance with the national performance will improve their teaching while preserving their autonomy. But in reality, making the link between local testing and national monitoring rests on devices which vitiate all these assumptions about the value of the operation.

The problem lies in the nature of item banking. If a national monitoring agency aims, as the APU does, to test the performance across the country of all children of a particular age in a particular area of the curriculum, some way has to be found of allowing for the varied experience of pupils in different schools. And if the survey results are to be compared validly from year to year, some way has to be found of updating the test items against a standard scale. Hence the tendency to establish a wide range of test items — an item bank — from which material can be drawn and into which new material can be inserted. Once such a bank has been established, it is tempting to argue that it can be used not only to feed items to national agencies, but also calibrate a further range of items for local use by authorities and schools.

The snag is that the way different pupils respond to a test item can depend on so many things — far too many to allow them all to be taken into account in calibrating them. What previous knowledge has the child acquired? What does he understand of it? How far is the test evidence of it? How far do home background, physical wellbeing, general cognitive understanding, social attitudes influence the result?

Some kind of assumptions must be made to reduce these factors to manageable proportions. The 'item domain' model for item banking assumes that items can be classified in terms of their technical characteristics. The 'latent trait' model assumes pupil performance depends on innate propensities or traits, and the Rasch model is the simplest of these. It assumes that items vary only according to their difficulty and a pupil's response depends only on his innate ability. It is attractive to researchers because items can then be calibrated using any group of pupils, without the need for large scale trials or representative samples required by other models. There are, however, three powerful objections to the Rasch model. First, the performance of a pupil on a given item may well depend on many factors, and not just on one supposed unidimensional trait. Second, the relative difficulty of items is not something absolute and unchanging, but will depend on pupils' exposure to different experiences and in particular to different teaching. And third, the model can only be made to work by selecting items which fit the model. The criterion is not their educational aptness but the degree to which they conform to a mathematical model.

It follows, therefore, that if these criticisms have any validity, not only is doubt cast, as discussed in the last chapter, on the results of the national APU tests: it is also arguable that attempts to extend the APU item bank to meet local needs will founder on the same grounds. For the critical step in connecting national testing levels to local items will be that of calibration, and this requires selection of items on the grounds of their educational usefulness to schools rather than their ability to fit the model. It is hypocrisy to pretend that the item bank allows teachers autonomy in selecting their own curriculum content if this is incompatible with the items on offer. Any item bank based on a latent trait model must constrain the choice of items, and the degree of constraint will be closer if it is to be standardised against a national system.

Given these serious problems, why did the APU decide right from the start that a link with local testing should be built into its terms of reference? Almost certainly, the extent of these problems was not appreciated at the time. The HMI and DES officials were content to accept the assurances of the NFER researchers that objective testing was not a dream but a reality, and that the technical problems could be overcome. The educational issues may well have been glossed over. This left the APU with three good reasons for advocating local links. First, there was the argument that LEAs would want to test anyway: better, therefore, to encourage them to use the APU tests, which would be superior to conventional standardised tests of reading and other 'basic skills'. And second, there was the enticing notion that the APU tests, suitably extended and tailored to local needs, would allow teachers to put a figure to every aspect of a pupil's performance. The system would triumph at last: the tiresome irregularities arising from human encounters between teachers and learners could be ironed out by a precise new mechanism. Finally, these performance figures could be directly associated with national norms, so that at a stroke the APU could both assess standards for the politicians and offer a diagnostic instrument to teachers. There was the risk of curriculum backwash, but if the APU tests came up to expectations, this effect could only be beneficial.

The arrangement had much to offer the NFER. As the APU's main testing contractor, it was paid to develop the mathematics and language tests, and (through its monitoring services unit) to administer and coordinate all the APU tests. By setting up an item bank and selling APU-compatible tests to local authorities, it would acquire the cachet of a national connection and strongly challenge other providers of tests and testing services in the UK. In May 1977, the NFER put forward the item bank proposal to a meeting of LEA representatives in London, and the result was 'overwhelming agreement that such a service would be useful and that the first subject areas in which materials should be developed should be mathematics and language' (NFER leaflet RI 80, May 1979). Specific items could be drawn from the bank, like books from a library: 'A user then only has to specify the details of the test he requires and appropriate questions can be drawn immediately from the bank to form such a test'. The tests would be useful 'for a wide range of different assessment applications, including screening ... diagnosing learning difficulties ... LEA surveys of attainment, and use by teachers for constructing attainment tests in specific topics'. A special feature would be the link with APU tests:

> With the permission of the DES it is intended that the Project item banks will be constructed in such a way that results obtained using tests designed for LEA survey purposes will be broadly compatible with performance measures presented in the APU reports.

In July 1980 I wrote to the director of this LEASIB project at the NFER (Dr Alan Willmott) and asked: will your item bank explicitly make use of APU validated tests as a means of validating the LEASIB tests? If so, what proportion of APU tests is being used in this way? He replied:

The actual detail of the linking exercise between the two banks is, of course, a technical problem. It is not a question of using APU tests but more of using a proportion of the items in the APU bank in order to be able to link the two banks statistically.

The distinction, though, between using APU tests and using APU items seems to be academic in the extreme. The APU is equally sensitive about the nature of the tie-up. I wrote in May 1980 to the administrative head of the APU (Miss D J Dawson) quoting the above passage from the NFER LEASIB leaflet about compatibility between the APU reports and the LEA tests, and drawing her attention to DES Report on Education 93, which states: 'The NFER propose to produce test material similar to that used for APU testing in mathematics, and in language, which will be made available to interested local education authorities'. I pointed out that while the light-sampling techniques of the APU testing will limit its backwash effect on school curricula, the use by LEAs of test material directly tied to APU material will promote a much closer link with the curriculum — particularly if blanket testing, to which some LEAs are committed, is employed. She replied:

> First, I must emphasise that the link between the APU item banks and those of the NFER's LEASIB project is minimal, and relates solely to the calibration of the items in the LEASIB banks with those in the APU bank so that the results from LEASIB testing will be expressible in terms broadly comparable with APU results. The banks of material are quite separate and consist of totally different items, i.e. items developed for use by the APU are not included either in their original form or in a modified form in NFER banks. The APU items are necessarily confidential ... If APU test items were to be freely available to local education authorities, there would be a possibility, as you recognise, of schools beginning to 'teach to the test', and this we are anxious to avoid.

But the link between the two item banks cannot be particularly 'minimal', since both must comply with the same Rasch model in all technical details, and the choice of LEASIB items must be governed by what will fit the APU model.

In any case, no decision about testing is value free. I put it to Dr Willmott that apart from the controversy over the Rasch model, the LEASIB project had further curriculum implications. It allows a link to be established between national norms and local practice, and thus implies models for the nature of learning and for curriculum outcomes. Did the NFER recognise these implications? He replied:

I would say that from the standpoint of LEASIB, I do not accept the implication you seem to be making that because there is an item bank this will come to dominate the curriculum ... Once LEASIB is established ... customers wanting a test will need to get down to the basics of what they want to test, and then put together a test to do the required task. My own feeling is that this exercise will be a useful exercise for many of those requiring tests and I think that this is preferable to schools and LEAs 'using the least worst test' off the shelf.

I find this reply unsatisfactory in two ways. First, all the effort of constructing a custom-built test cannot disguise the fact that the items which make it up are validated against APU norms, and so its results will be interpreted in terms of those norms. And second, I find it difficult to see who, apart from LEAs, will be requiring these special tests. Teachers in schools are hardly likely to be able to afford them, since 'counselling at the outset — in terms of discussing with the customer the kind of test material that is required — is probably going to be the single most important stage in the whole exercise' (Willmott, 1980). This will be a costly affair. Further, few teachers will be able (or, indeed, wish) to specify their objectives with such rigour and detail as to form the recipe for a item-banked test. I conclude, therefore, that the LEASIB facility will be a device enabling LEAs to buy tests broadly similar to APU tests so that they can apply them, possibly on a blanket basis, to their schools and so monitor standards and reinforce LEA guidelines.

I put it to Miss Dawson that in allowing NFER access to APU tests for its LEASIB project, the APU was negating its declared intention to monitor, rather than influence the curriculum. Would it not therefore be logical for the APU to embargo all its test material, and so eliminate the inconsistency in the APU position? She replied:

The APU has been concerned from the start to keep its influence on the school curriculum to a minimum ... The APU does not seek to assess individual pupils' performance. A number of local education authorities are, however, interested in comparing the performance of pupils in their own schools with the APU's national performance figures and have asked the NFER (which, as you will know, is funded by the local education authorities) to develop comparable test materials. It would seem to be to the advantage of the education service as a whole that local assessment, if and when it takes place, should be consistent both within and between different local education authorities. Obviously, the conditions under which the NFER materials are made available to local education authorities and ultimately to schools will be for the NFER and the local education authorities to decide.

The argument seems to be: whatever we in the APU might think, it is a fact that many LEAs are hell-bent on testing. If they choose to ask the NFER for more and more tests, we can hardly stop them, since they run the outfit. And if there must be more tests, they might as well all be comparable. As for the use LEAs make of the tests, that's their affair, and no fault of ours.

I think that those who care about the quality of education in our schools will find the entire LEASIB operation exceedingly disturbing. A great deal needs to be done to the curriculum of our primary and secondary schools, as the HMI national surveys have confirmed. The need is for whole curriculum planning based in the schools themselves, reflecting the most careful discussion about educational issues and extensive in-service support linked to the resolution and implementation of curriculum problems. The evidence shows that there is no case whatever for further emphasis on basic skills: the danger is rather that pupils may be offered an impoverished curriculum because of an undue emphasis on what can be readily drilled and tested. Neither is there a case for imposing curriculum change by means of tests: monitoring instruments and cobbled-up guidelines are no substitute for curriculum planning. But what they can do is obstruct it — by side-stepping fundamental questions of educational value.

The LEASIB project would represent a grave threat if it were conducted by a totally independent agency, like a university department of education. It is that much more serious a threat because it is, in effect, run by the LEAs themselves. The NFER's monopoly position in the two basic areas of language and mathematics has now been further extended: despite bids from such reputable modern language departments as that at York University, the NFER has been awarded the contract for developing the APU modern language tests. And by allowing the NFER to tap the APU bank and so calibrate its own commercial item bank, the APU has compromised its avowed intention to minimise curriculum backwash. Yet had it not declared a link with local testing to be one of its basic tasks, the APU might not have fulfilled the political requirements which gave it birth. It is consequently in a cleft stick, and can now do little but stand on the sidelines and wring its hands.

Undoubtedly, too, the LEASIB project will open up the testing market still further. A significant development here stems from the decision of the NFER's publishing offshoot to solve its financial problems by linking with a commercial publisher. This means that the LEASIB tests — which result from national APU norms — may be marketed not by the publishing company of a research foundation but by an alliance between the publishing company and a commercial publishing house. Three issues arise. First, the NFER as a research foundation would doubtless allow other research bodies and testing agencies to use its technical data and so validate other tests against the LEASIB item bank, or allow others to take advantage of the experience gained by the NFER in constructing the APU materials. But there could conceivably be a conflict of interest between free academic access and the opportunity thus offered to potential competitors in the commercial marketing of tests. Second, in providing such access, the Research Foundation might find itself in breach of undertakings to the DES to respect APU confidentiality: such confidentiality would be built in to the key LEASIB operation of developing tests for LEAs that are 'broadly compatible' with APU norms of performance. Third, active promotion of LEASIB tests by NFER–Nelson may stimulate commercial competition, leading to a proliferation of other tests emulating the APU/NFER originals. The APU hoped, in linking with the NFER, to standardise monitoring instruments: the outcome may be an even greater variety of tests.

There are, however, some signs that teachers have begun to realise the dangers of monitoring. It is reported (*The Times Educational Supplement*, 8 February 1980) that although a representative sample of 650 schools was selected for the 1979 APU mathematics tests of fifteen year olds, thirty-eight schools refused to take part and thirty did not reply. And in April 1978, the NUT advised its local associations and divisions that:

> The Union will support divisions opposed to the imposition of local authority testing across entire age groups. Subject to the approval of the Action Committee, the Union would support divisions in a policy of non-cooperation and opposition by Union members.

The refusal of schools to take part in the APU sample testing is a welcome indication that heads and staff are appreciating that the result of monitoring is, ultimately, a diminished curriculum. Blanket testing is even more odious an imposition: all testing corrupts, and absolute testing corrupts absolutely. But in some ways the linking of local testing with national monitoring — whether on a sample or blanket basis — is the most pernicious development of all. For it will further reinforce a production model of schooling, which is implicit in the APU formulation but which cannot take full effect until it is geared to local control and school practice. The LEASIB project provides the missing mechanism. It behoves teachers, parents and all who seek to make the curriculum a broad and coherent reflection of our culture to be alert to the threat posed by national and local attempts to evaluate school performance.

NOTES

1 **William Tyndale School.** In 1974 a new head was appointed to William Tyndale Junior School, Islington, London, and methods were introduced which largely allowed pupils to decide their own activities. Within six months there was conflict within the staff of the school, and the head of the neighbouring Infants School complained about 'disruption and bad behaviour of the Junior School children' (Auld, 1976). The ILEA divisional inspector presented a confidential report on the school to its Managers (the governors of the school), and in 1975 a petition, drafted by one of the governors, was circulated calling on the ILEA 'to take urgent steps to re-establish public confidence in the Junior School'. After the Managers had been barred from visiting the school during school hours, they asked the ILEA for a DES inspection of the school. By July 1975 the ILEA had agreed to set up its own Public Inquiry into the school, chaired by Robin Auld, QC. The Inquiry ended in February 1976, after calling 100 witnesses and addressing 600 documents. Subsequently the chairman of the ILEA Schools Sub-Committee resigned, as did the school's managers; and the teachers faced disciplinary proceedings.

The William Tyndale affair is of profound importance in any study of the governance and politics of education, and raises key issues regarding the rights of children, teachers, parents, governors and LEA officers and members in determining the character of a school's educational programme.

2 **Hawthorne, halo and Matthew effects.** The Hawthorne effect (named after some experiments conducted in an American factory in the 1920s) suggests that a newly introduced change will itself bring about an improvement in performance, simply because it is a change from routine. The halo effect means that those responsible for some innovation are regarded with particular approbation, and are thereafter given favourable consideration. The Matthew principle acknowledges that change often benefits those who are already blessed, so their performance improves even more — to him that hath shall be given.

5 Self Evaluation in Schools

The last three chapters have looked at ways in which the performance of schools can be evaluated from outside, and from above: by external agencies (NAEP, state boards, the APU, LEAs) which represent the interests of those to whom the school is in some way responsible. The focus has been on ways in which the consequences of decisions made by teachers and schools can be assessed — on examination results, reading test results, standardised test scores, APU tests of pupil performance. All this could be termed *output evaluation*, and this is the obvious strategy for any outsider wishing to know more about a complex mechanism. It answers the question: 'What is coming out of all this?' and implies that those asking the question have a right to know. On the whole this form of evaluation has been little challenged, although in one local authority where the teachers' professional associations are strongly represented on the education committee, the adviser responsible for evaluation told me: 'The teacher representatives were not convinced of the virtues of blanket testing, and the school psychologists opposed it too. Given the LEASIB scheme we felt light sampling was important, but the teachers had doubts about item banking and didn't like it.'

But an attraction of output evaluation is that it offers a *measure* of an activity which is otherwise hard to penetrate, and this is attractive to administrators and advisers and can seem seductive to teachers. Also, in confining evaluation to external evidence it is easier for the evaluating authority to argue that it does not wish to be intrusive. But the difficulty is that any attempt to measure outputs or products of education distorts and interferes with what is measured, so the promise of objectivity is unfulfilled: 'In America, the political consequences of admitting that the (NAEP) tests "do not test what they were supposed to test" were too damaging in view of the expensive nature of the operation' (Galton, 1979). This realisation has yet to dawn in the UK.

Another way in which a controlling institution can examine the work of its subsidiaries is by asking a rather different question: 'How does this place function?' Instead of imposing output measures on the subordinate, it asks for an account of how it sets about its tasks.

This might be termed *procedural evaluation*. The favoured device is the checklist, possibly combined with a formal report. This avoids the problem of measures associated with output evaluation, but it does so by intruding more overtly on the inner mechanism of the school. It accepts a more qualitative style of evaluation and the attendant problems of interpretation, but by emphasising the self-evaluative nature of the exercise it may be possible to tone down the political problems arising from a more explicit interference with how a school works. This approach to self-evaluation will be examined in the next section.

The logical extension of this idea is *process evaluation*, which asks the question: 'How do things happen?' This is much closer to a research orientation, and it will be no surprise that this approach is attractive to the academic community. Thus, in deciding how to carry out 'a study in secondary schooling', Weston (1979) concludes:

> The relevant question was not: 'how are they doing?' but 'what is happening?' If there was going to be evaluation it was in the sense of making connections between the intentions, values and expectations of all those involved in the complex process of teaching and learning ... and relating them to the context in which the process took place.

Harlen (1978) sees this kind of activity as an appropriate and necessary part of the teacher's role:

> Wholly external evaluation, of the 'payment by results' kind leaves teachers little freedom to make decisions about their work; the greater the degree of participation by teachers in evaluation the more freedom they have to decide appropriate goals for their pupils and experiences through which these can be achieved.

This is the full floruit of evaluation: what started off as a retrospective look at past decisions suddenly is transformed into a way in which teachers can 'decide appropriate goals'. This view of evaluation has implications both for curriculum and for pedagogy, and it forms the springboard for a number of research departures which I shall review in the subsequent section. But it also appeals to administrators, since it argues that by encouraging schools to engage in self-evaluation, they will establish 'a forum for acknowledging and debating values in education' (Harlen, 1978) and so, one might presume, go on to develop new and better styles of curriculum activity. In the last two sections of this chapter I shall look first at a case study of a self-evaluation exercise in a school, and then look more closely at the assumptions on which these approaches to evaluation rest.

School Self Evaluation

A number of local authorities have responded to calls for greater accountability and monitoring of school performance by devising self-evaluation instruments for use by schools, or by urging the adoption of such instruments. This activity of school self evaluation now has its own abbreviation (SSE), and it appears that teachers have played a willing part in developing it and have been persuaded to overcome any misgivings about using it. Several LEA schemes have been published, but as yet there are few published results of SSE in schools.

A useful survey of the field, which includes a valuable bibliography of English and American publications, has been produced by Gordon Elliott (1980) in association with the Schools Council. Elliott's survey disclosed 'a clear indication of thinking and activity that seemed to suggest the beginnings of *a movement*'. He concluded that 'Because it is so recent self-evaluation has not received the attention other aspects of the accountability movement have attracted. But it is potentially more important than all the others'. No less than 'A minimum of five thousand schools have been circulated with checklists and guidelines' (Elliott, 1981), and no less than twenty-one local authorities have produced SSE schemes of some kind or other.

Without doubt, the mainspring for all this activity has been accountability rather than any rationale for evaluation in purely educational terms: 'In both the theoretical and practical sense it was evident that accountability was an important issue' (Elliott, 1980). Furthermore, Elliott notes that 'a particular model of curriculum evaluation — the objectives model — is central to all the twenty-one schemes that were examined'. It is thus all too easy for a proposal which starts off with the notion that schools should give an account of what they are doing, in response to a checklist of objectives-based questions, to turn into a device for making schools accountable to higher authority in certain specified respects.

A brief look at three of the published schemes will indicate the direction SSE is taking. A seminal scheme has been that of the Inner London Education Authority, which in 1977 launched a booklet entitled *Keeping the School under Review*: 'A method of self-assessment for schools devised by the ILEA inspectorate'. ILEA schools have been encouraged to make use of it:

> Two years on, and after some vigorous salesmanship by the inspectorate, which seems to have overcome the initial suspicions of the

teachers' unions, the booklet has been made more or less welcome ... especially perhaps in secondary schools where the more complex organisational problems lend themselves more easily to formal evaluation. (O' Connor, 1979)

The scheme was the work of ILEA staff inspectors with a group of head teachers: the impetus came from outside individual schools, and the evaluation is not entirely a matter for schools. O'Connor quotes an ILEA inspector as hoping that 'schools who take into use a form of self-assessment will be prepared to discuss the outcomes with colleagues in the inspectorate'. This sounds rather like the police formula of inviting suspects to help them with their inquiries. The booklet has ambitious aims: not only to 'help schools make explicit some principles and practices of their work which have not always been consciously appreciated', but also to 'question them and to establish priorities for the future'. It is plainly seen, then, as a device for promoting curriculum planning. Again, it is assumed that scrutinising existing practice will promote reform, despite Flynn's point (1972) that an evaluation can only consider evidence of what is or what has been — not of what might be.

After a short opening section listing the statistical information which schools would normally collect about themselves — numbers of parents making the school their choice, of pupils receiving uniform grants, of teacher-day sickness absences; public examinatiom results, attendance rates, staff mobility, cost of furniture repairs during the year — the booklet turns out to be a very long checklist of questions. These are arranged under twelve headings: for example, under 'the school environment', teachers are asked: 'How would one describe the noise level, and the kind of noise, at various times and places?' Under 'decision-making and communications', one finds: 'Are there adequate opportunities for all members of staff to express their views?' Heads are urged to ask themselves: 'How often did I ... go to a school gate at the beginning or end of school? ... Does every person in the school know to whom he or she is immediately responsible and for what?'

Simons (1980a) has noted three disadvantages of the checklist approach to evaluation. First, 'Once checks have been made the information still has to be dealt with'. Second, 'They do not adequately reflect the complexity of knowledge (teachers) have about the pupils or the school'. Third, how is the information to be used to develop new strategies? 'Some strategy for its use was seen by the schools to be needed.' It will be noted, too, that the ILEA checklist essentially peddles indicators of performance, and that these frequently imply value judgments. It is implicit that heads ought to spend their time watching the school gates; that all members of staff should be free to express their views on any subject; that any ambiguities about role definition should be eradicated. These may, or may not, be desirable attributes in a school; the point is that their desirability is taken for granted and seen as the standard by which the LEA would seek to judge its schools. One might argue that these implied values could be made overt by inviting staff to respond to the questions in particular ways. But no advice is offered on how responses should be couched, and indeed most such schemes make a virtue of the open-ended nature of the questions asked. Given the prescriptive intent of the questions, any attempt to give guidance on how to answer them might well be seen as too directive.

In the event, the ILEA document provoked hostility for a time from teachers' organisations when it turned out that school governors had begun to ask heads to include the replies to *Keeping the School under Review* in their governors' reports. The line between information obtained in order to give a professional account, and its use to enable those in authority to pass judgment — to hold accountable — is very easily crossed. All such schemes run this risk: the good intentions of LEA inspectors and advisers in setting up SSE schemes can look like a devious plot for tighter political control. G. Elliott (1980) sets the ILEA scheme in the context of adverse publicity in the wake of the William Tyndale affair (Auld, 1976), and sees it as 'a very brave attempt to strike a balance between restoring the public's confidence in ILEA and giving the authority's teachers a vote of confidence'.

The difficulty, indeed, in judging any of these SSE schemes originating from outside the school is that while the professional integrity of those responsible for introducing them is never in question, the schemes may well reap a harvest of unexpected and undesirable consequences. On the face of it, the second scheme I shall mention — that adopted by Oxfordshire — appears particularly prescriptive. In addition to a checklist document substantially the same as the ILEA original — this indebtedness is acknowledged by the Oxfordshire CEO, Tim Brighouse, who came to the post from ILEA — a second SSE strategy is in force. Every four years each school must present a confidential report to its governors, prepared by the head 'with help from the advisory services and other such lay or professional involvement external to the school as may be appropriate'. The report is then forwarded along with the governors' comments 'to Schools' sub-committee in confidential session' (Brighouse, 1979). Sterne (1980) points out that the reporting system has been agreed 'with the headteachers' associations, and it has been introduced to each school after a visit from the chief education officer' The authority specifies eight separate sections for the four-yearly school report, and enough further detail is given to leave little room for doubt about what the authority deems to be important. 'Each section should not only be descriptive but also include evaluative comment', and items specified include:

the provision of a basic curriculum for the first three years, giving breadth of experience and variety of study method, together with the opportunity of additional study for the more able, and supportive help for the least able;

the school's system of sanctions; recognition of pupil achievement;

a balanced curriculum for each pupil; an appropriate option system; a whole school policy of evaluation of its curriculum;

own school testing against APU/use of other tests;

management techniques;

links with industry.

Clearly a school reporting scheme as detailed as this — and associated with a procedure which takes the report up to the education committee — cannot be separated from the issue of school accountability. It is well known that whereas prior to local government reorganisation in 1974, Oxfordshire had a tradition for educational innovation and devolved school autonomy, its members have since shown an enthusiasm for *dirigisme* and zeal in applying financial cuts. Evaluation schemes of this kind are on all fours with this change of face, where schools become satellite units subordinate to the aims and attitudes of the centre. What purports to be self evaluation is in fact a device for strengthening central control and for making value judgments about education and curriculum which have traditionally been made at the periphery as well as at the centre.

Even so, much can depend on how such schemes work out in practice, and the latitude given to schools in making their reports. In a press account of the reporting process in an Oxfordshire secondary school (*The Times Educational Supplement*, 13 February 1981), the CEO sees it as 'A form of governor education', and the deputy head found it 'very profitable ... The head has used this to get things done

for the school'. It is, of course, always in doubt how far such reports
will confine themselves to the school as it stands — and to what extra
resources are needed so that existing things may be done better —
and how far they will promote reflection on new ideas and procedures. It is easy to claim that SSE devices of this kind lead to a new
sensitivity towards change on the part of staff; in practice, the reports
might merely foster self-justification rather than self-evaluation. And
though they may be an effective way of demonstrating to governors
and members that schools do good work and need more funds, a
price is paid: the principle is explicit that schools cannot be trusted to
do a good job without rendering a formal account of the job they
have done. Perhaps this is an inevitable consequence of accountability pressures; but it must be recognised not only as a restrictive view
of teacher professionalism, but as a procedure which, of necessity,
shifts power from the periphery to the centre.

A third SSE scheme makes its prescriptive, objectives-based nature
much more explicit than either of those discussed already. In
Solihull, the scheme sets before subject teachers in secondary schools
a list of statements intended 'to assist teachers to evaluate their own
effectiveness as a subject teacher', but which can also be used 'to
record their own views on the quality of support and advice received
from Heads of Department'. Under the heading 'Objectives, planning and preparation', we find such statements as:

> I have a clear and comprehensive set of objectives, specifying
> knowledge and skills and values to be acquired, for each unit of work;

> My objectives are expressed in terms of measurable outcomes which
> are reflected in the testing and assessment procedures for each unit of
> work;

> My objectives are linked to the reporting/evaluating systems, which
> are designed to facilitate the monitoring of pupils' progress towards
> objectives.

This is plainly an extreme example of managerialism applied to
education, and its authors must be unaware of the mediocrity to
which similar objectives-inspired exercises have led in the US. I have
worked with a number of talented teachers in secondary schools, and
I am certain that none of them would be able to offer 'a clear and
comprehensive set of objectives, specifying knowledge and skills and
values to be acquired', let alone be prepared to express them in
measurable form. And as a head, it would have been not merely an
impertinence to make such a request, but an acknowledgment that

my understanding of the process of education was totally wrong-headed.

The Solihull scheme also includes an 'evaluation response sheet' which includes 'a rating for importance or priority and a rating for effectiveness'. At a conference at which this scheme was discussed (Sterne, 1980), a head commented that in using the Solihull document,

> there was not sufficient focus on the pupil and on educational benefits to the pupil ... The questions implied sets of answers ... The document gives no guidance on the management process in the school.

An industrial training manager thought 'the document was so very comprehensive that it might ... be too difficult to use'.

There is nothing particularly difficult about compiling lists of performance indicators. But any such list makes assumptions and implies judgments — all evaluation is political. What is left out, and what is put in, reflect the values of the compilers and their own construction of normative school performance. 'When did you last have a drink in the local pub?' is a question which might have a great deal to do with teachers' attitudes towards each other and the school's view of the community, and it could bear on the school's commitment to curriculum innovation. But it doesn't fit in with the managerial stereotype of 'effectiveness', which generally means some sort of procedural efficiency.

All the schemes discussed here are essentially concerned with what I have termed *procedural* evaluation — with attempts to get the school to describe how it functions. Yet a number of the questions cited are addressed to individual teachers, and therefore slide into an evaluation of *process* — of how teachers make decisions and see themselves. As G. Elliott puts it (1981): 'The focus of self-evaluation in England and Wales has been the school rather than the individual teacher. Inevitably, however, when evaluating an institution you cannot escape saying something about individuals'. He points out that from March 1980, the *Thesaurus of E.R.I.C. Descriptors* (a computerised North American index of educational references) has eliminated the terms *self appraisal, self assessment* and *self evaluation*, in favour of two categories: *self evaluation (groups)*, meaning 'asssessment of an institution, organisation, programme etc. by its members or sponsors', and *self evaluation (individuals)*, meaning 'individuals' assessment of themselves' (G. Elliott, 1980).

In current British usage, SSE includes both forms of self evaluation. The pressure of school accountability has given it an institu-

tional focus, but the judgments of individual teachers on themselves
— and on other staff — will be an element of published evaluations or
reports. Two important issues arise. First, what guarantees of confidentiality should be secured by self-evaluating schools? It should be
borne in mind, too, that confidences can easily be breached in a
political climate which seeks to open the decision making process to a
wider public. Thus Salford primary teachers were assured in 1980
that their SSE reports would be confidential to officers and education
committee members, and were therefore presented to the committee
as such. But since the committee meetings are public, the reports
were the subject of press coverage.

Second, SSE strategies mean that judgments by staff on their
work and that of other teachers are available to those who determine
their promotion in an authority — to its advisers, officers and members. In the days when teachers were hard to get and it was easy to
win promotion in another authority, a teacher could set out to do his
best for his school without worrying too much about any conflict between what was right for his school, and whatever pet ideas the LEA
advisers might try to advance. The reference from his own head
teacher would justify his efforts. But now, with falling school rolls
obliging most LEAs to put a 'ring fence' around their territory, promotion is more likely to come within the authority itself. How
honest, therefore, should a teacher be about his own failings, knowing that they can be identified by the senior adviser for secondary
schools, who will sit on the interview board when he applies for a
deputy headship at the school down the road? How much validity, in
fact, can be attached to SSE exercises which are inspired from outside
the school, and what risks does a school and a staff run in baring its
soul to those who are the gatekeepers for professional advancement?
Or — to put the question a little more gently — does not SSE place
information in the hands of advisers and officers which puts an impossible strain on their capacity for detached judgment?

It is clear that SSE is a much more complex and fraught undertaking than would be evident from the zeal with which checklists of
questions and objectives have been assembled and circulated. And in
any event, what is the true cost of SSE? I recall that some years ago,
Messrs Marks and Spencer calculated the true cost of writing a letter
and immediately simplified their paperwork throughout the organisation. The cost in meetings, report writing, agonising and final
presentation of SSE must be staggering. A simple calculation shows
that in Oxfordshire, with four hundred schools each writing a report
every four years, two reports will be generated every week as a con-

tinuous process. Should this colossal investment in the time of highly paid teachers, heads, advisers and officers be devoted to writing reports on what has already happened, or on support strategies for school based curriculum development aimed at improving the quality of decisions before things happen?

The next section will look more closely at the self evaluation of individuals which must form a part of SSE. But it is worth remarking here that quite apart from the reservations I have mentioned, it does not follow that we can learn about ourselves in the same way we learn about others. The step from observing the outputs of school actions to forms of self-observation is easily taken, once one has succumbed to the checklist view of education which is currently fashionable. But, as Clark (1979) has pointed out in an important paper which challenges the behavioural assumptions underlying so many of these approaches, the step is not a logical one:

> At the back of the belief that one can eventually learn to 'modify' one's own behaviour lies the mistake of assuming that one comes to know about oneself ... in exactly the way as one comes to know about others — by observation ... One's descriptions of one's own current actions are not normally based on observation. They are not verified at all but, rather, decided upon. It follows, then, that the assumption that one controls one's own behaviour in the same way as one controls that of others ... must be false.

Above all, the disturbing thing about the fashion for school 'self audit' or self evaluation is the assumption that a good school is one which uses the right mechanisms or routines. The value judgments seem to take second place to the functionalism of schooling. A book on self evaluation opens with this explicit emphasis on technique rather than reasoning:

> This book is about ways of making schools more effective and about ways of ensuring that they are seen to be effective. It is not about the ends of education... The concern here is with means not ends, or how to do it more effectively rather than what to do. (Shipman, 1979).

The objectives-based scheduling used in North America in the 1960s by the Rand Corporation is instanced as an example of 'a systematic approach (which) makes it certain that objectives, teaching programmes, and evaluation itself are open to continuous feedback and hence change'. These systems-based models are now widely discredited not only when transplanted to education (see, for example, Macdonald-Ross, 1975) but also in the industrial context which spawned them

(PPBS, or planned programme budgeting system, are seen as mechanism rather than people-centred, and have never been used by the UK's most successful industrial company, GEC). The behaviourist basis of Shipman's approach is evident from his emphasis on the fragmentation of aims into specific objectives:

> There is no need to agonize too long over philosophical matters of aims. The need is for a set of working objectives that can focus evaluation. The objectives establish a tactical position that can enable the staff to get on with evaluation.

What matters, it seems, is not taking care to decide why one acts in a certain way, but to choose actions which can most readily be evaluated. The means are justifying the ends, just as they must in the Rasch model for item banking — only items which fit the model can be chosen. What matters is not developing an understanding of one's role, but deploying analytical techniques for describing it in differentiated terms. Shipman quotes Poster (1976) with approval: 'The teacher's role *is* capable of definition. In the complex structures of our secondary schools that definition is necessary, if each of us is ever to walk his way through the maze of priorities'.

The weakness with Shipman's book is that it is based on the fallacy that, in education, means can be divorced from ends. For values are implicit in every educational act, and there is no 'objective' or 'systematic' way in which the quality of an act can be separated from the way it is performed. But Shipman chooses to deny this imperative, in order to express schooling as a set of black and white outputs:

> The choice is between leaving evaluation to impressions that have no necessarily consistent or even detectable frame of reference, or organizing it so that the criteria of success and failure are spelled out. It is a choice between casual and systematic judgement. (Shipman, 1979)

But, of course, judgment can be systematic — based on some rationale of education — without for one moment obliging teachers or administrators to spell out 'criteria of success and failure'. My experience of whole school curriculum innovation suggests that nothing would have guaranteed disaster more certainly than an emphasis on systematic criteria of success or failure. Shipman presents a view of curriculum process which is not only illogical and misleading — it will do nothing to promote whole curriculum change, and can only foster a serious misconception of what education should be about.

Self Evaluation and Teacher Professionalism

Since the late 1960s there has been a trend on both sides of the Atlantic to see evaluation as 'big science' — a separate element in the curriculum process with its own specialists, the 'evaluators'. The next step is to make 'evaluation' an academic sub-field in its own right, and then extend its influence by arguing that teachers must be initiated into its own arcane rites. And although this territorial annexation is essentially an academic industry, it has been enormously helped by the political instabilities of the sixties and seventies. The more hard-nosed the administration, the more readily has it funded evaluation and monitoring programmes in the hope of producing objective performance data. Hence the follies of NAEP and the APU, and of local education authorities in both countries. The mechanistic techniques described in the previous section are in the same tradition, and suffer from the same fatal flaw: 'The crucial criticism of the objectives model is that it assesses without explaining ... Hence the developer of curriculum cannot learn from it' (Stenhouse, 1975).

The reaction to this scientific/psychometric model was a call for a more holistic or interpretive style of evaluation, one which would look not for simple single-outcome measures of complex events, but for both intended and unintended consequences of actions rooted in particular contexts: evaluation 'orientated to the complex and dynamic nature of education, one which gives proper attention to the diverse purposes and judgments of the practitioner' (Stake, 1967). The effect of such evaluation is that 'Instead of discriminating between alternative courses of action, it seeks to make actors more discriminating' (Stenhouse, 1980). The move from objectives-based to context-based evaluation takes us from the product to the process, and to the teachers and the schools where the drama is acted out.

It also offers the opportunity to see curriculum process as a whole. The classic Bloom-Taba-Tyler objectives model used for so many American curriculum development projects lent itself to separate roles for the researcher/designer, field diffuser and team evaluator. But for Stenhouse (1975), 'The existence of the evaluator implies the existence of the developer, another role of which I am sceptical. I want to argue against the separation of developer and evaluator and in favour of integrated curriculum research'. This line of thought led Stenhouse to advocate 'research-based teaching', and so another reason emerges for encouraging teachers to adopt reflexive, self-evaluative roles as an explicit aspect of their professionalism. As

Elliott puts it (1978), 'evaluations of teaching are appropriately based on the study of what is actually happening in that teaching situation'. One result was developments like the Ford Teaching Project, offering teachers 'a method of self-evaluation within a democratic-professional system of classroom accountability'. Classroom research of this kind seeks to identify teachers' actions and assess their consequences. Other classroom researchers aim at nothing less than a socio-technology of teaching: 'classroom studies seek an understanding of the characteristics of the environments within which particular methods or approaches to instruction both come about and affect student learning' (Westbury, 1979).

What has happened, in effect, is that the concept of evaluation has been steadily expanded in order to expose ever richer seams to the researchers' picks and shovels. For Tyler (1949), evaluation was 'essentially the process of determining to what extent the educational objectives are actually being realised by the programme of curriculum and instruction'. But once we understand that data about pupil behaviour are a poor basis for educational decisions (a state yet to be reached, it seems, by the DES and many LEAs), we are forced to think again:

> The broadening of the concept of evaluation, to bring the school and all who work in the educational system into its compass, the raising of questions about who is the evaluation for, what is it for and who carries it out, have presented evaluation as a complex process in which many issues are unresolved ... All this could be taken as an argument for saying that the variables are so many and so interconnected that evaluation is unlikely to be of use. In this book the opposite conclusion has been drawn, that the complexity of the problems requires more evaluation activity, not less. (Harlen, 1978)

I would wish, however, to refute this conclusion, and to argue that the concept of evaluation is too fragile, indeterminate and ultimately inappropriate to bear such a weight of curriculum speculation. The complexity of the problems requires a great deal less evaluation, and a great deal more emphasis on how teachers should define and solve curriculum issues rather than on the results of curriculum activity.

It is necessary, though, to look at some of these well-meaning attempts to achieve curriculum renewal by means of evaluative probes. A case-study approach which avoids the objectives-based productivity models underlying the methods of the previous section, and which instead draws on responsive or illuminative styles of evaluation, has been described by Simons (1980b). The aim is:

...to study the processes of teaching, learning and schooling ... And one of the best ways to represent and promote understanding of these processes is to accumulate and make available detailed descriptions of teaching and learning and the values and effects of curriculum policies within the context of particular schools and classrooms.

School self evaluation is 'educational and professional', and 'evaluation should precede curriculum development and not follow in its wake'. The evaluation takes the form of small-scale observation of the particular: teachers and evaluators will 'record events in progress, document observations'. The process takes time: Simons ran a course for twelve teachers in a school over twenty weeks, and found 'some period of immersion in the evaluation role is required ... Teachers lack a precise enough language through which they can share their professional concerns'.

This approach to school self evaluation is, I think, thoughtful and enlightened and of a very different cast from that advocated by those who would separate educational means from ends. It is worth noting, in fact, that Simons found teachers all too ready to deskill themselves when required to undertake formal styles of evaluation: 'they seek a corresponding formality in the means of data collection and analysis' and as a result overlook the need to extend their skills and practices and make more informed judgments. I am sure, too, that case studies of this kind can be a valuable way of interpreting the processes of schools — I have already referred in this book to a similar American study (Denny, 1977). But as Simons says, 'Subjective judgments are an important part of the process'. A case study is only as good as those judgments, and good studies are not notably abundant.

I have, though, two reservations about this style of evaluation. First, I am doubtful about the proposition that 'evaluation should precede curriculum development', not least because I share Stenhouse's distaste for separating evaluation from development. My experience of school-based curriculum innovation is that teachers do not see this as a natural separation; their decision to embark on a new course of action embodies their appreciation of their existing experience in a much more integral fashion, and one which may not lend itself to the kinds of instruments used by Simons to dissect it. And even if such a separation is made and an evaluation carried out so as to provide what Eisner (1975) has called a 'thick description' of school events, I am unconvinced that this will itself lead on to curriculum development. It may merely result in a refurbishment of the status quo. Reid (1978) puts his finger on the missing link:

The move from psychometric paradigms to concepts of 'illumination' and 'portrayal' offers the promise of sensitive and wide-ranging studies of educational practice. Researchers have, however, been less ready to grasp the nettle of connecting practice with the decisions that produced it and to ask, 'Was this the right thing to do?' or 'Was this an appropriate way to go about identifying the problem, proposing solutions and judging which one should be developed?'

Responsive evaluation studies can be useful in themselves, but if curriculum change is our objective (and there seems little other reason for evaluating) then we might much more profitably start at the connection 'between styles of decision-making and curricular outcomes' (Reid, 1978). The elaborate evaluation exercises may amount only to an expensive and time-consuming way of muddying the waters.

Second, I doubt whether such exercises will enhance the confidence of teachers to strike out on new paths. They may have a better understanding of their own worries and inadequacies, and this may help them improve what is done already. But, as Simons (1980b) points out,

> Opening one's policies and practices to critique in a system characterised by privacy for so long can be a challenging but threatening exercise. What was once implicit now becomes explicit. What was once informal ... now becomes an accepted part of the school's agenda for study.

Certainly teachers should be encouraged to reflect on their familiar assumptions. But need this be such a threatening, intra-personal affair? Erlandson (1973) observes: 'Yes: evaluation in education is a wonderful thing — at least from the viewpoint of the person doing the evaluating ... Evaluation is something that someone does to someone else'. It may well be that some implicit activities are better left that way. There is little point in a view of professionalism which, in the pursuit of openness and the explicit, undermines the risky personal initiative on which good teaching so often depends.

A less ambitious approach to school self-evaluation concentrates on teachers' assessments of their lessons and pupils' responses. Such approaches have been reviewed by Galton (1979):

> Typically teachers are brought together and asked to state what skills they expect pupils to use during the course of a lesson. They are asked to indicate what kinds of evidence would be acceptable in support of these expectations. Gradually, through discussion, a consensus emerges within the group and different criteria can then be listed and classified ... Checklists are then developed and pupils rated after obser-

vation ... The process by which teachers acquire such skills tends to be somewhat drawn out.

Galton refers to three published studies in which attempts to persuade other schools to adopt teacher-group checklists have 'not so far met with much success'. It takes so much time to learn how to use the checklists, teachers feel 'that this can be better spent doing other things with their pupils'. Galton considers these approaches should be pursued despite these difficulties, with more in-service work on the technique of assessment and a 'less directed style of teaching':

> In the past researchers developing these new assessment techniques have tended to be over ambitious. Both the Scottish 'Pupils in Profile' and Wynne Harlen's 'Progress in Learning Science' checklists are far too comprehensive and elaborate. Both look impracticable and time consuming so that natural resistance ... is built in from the start.

The fact is, though, that the word 'checklist' is a guarantee that the reductionists have been at work. Whether the list is long or short or behavioural or not, consensus devices have been used to boil down complex judgements into portable catechisms. The need in curriculum planning is not for consensus, but for a new synthesis: to devise ways of decision-making which are not distillations of existing practice, but which build on practice to frame new solutions. It seems vain to hope that devices of this kind will themselves lead to changes in teaching styles: how teachers teach is a function of their view of themselves — of their attitudes towards society and their interpretation of our culture. An approach through evaluation seems to me a misconception of the scale and nature of what change of this kind involves. Yet if we are talking about curriculum change, we are talking about these quite fundamental issues and we must devise appropriate ways of tackling them. Compiling checklists does not seem to me to be one of them.

This kind of evaluation research blurs into classroom interaction research, a field which has been vigorously tilled in the USA but which has yet to bear much fruit. W. Taylor (1978) notes that by 1970, one compilation of American instruments — 'tests, schedules, category systems used ... to explore the interaction of teachers and pupils in classrooms' — filled sixteen volumes. Ten years on, the amount (and cost) of all this labour does not bear contemplating. It results, in Taylor's words, from 'The desire of social scientists to look beneath the surface of things, to unmask, to de-mythologise, to disenchant, to open up hitherto "privatised" activities for investigation'. It is also easy research to do, because the classroom is a self-contained unit, the literature is accessible, and the process under investigation so complex that it is difficult to dispute any conclusion, however trivial or misconceived. This is a field which is long on description, but short on theory. Taylor notes 'the paucity of theory about teacher education', and 'its relatively poor quality'.

In the early seventies classroom research languished, partly because of its doubtful value, but partly also because of disenchantment with psychometric styles of evaluation. Classroom research is evaluation of teacher activity, and most of it relies on an objective-based output model of classroom process. Just as with psychometric attempts to define pupil performance in terms of observed responses, it became obvious to many that to describe, but not to explain, can be unwise as well as unhelpful. As with test scores, the defined output states will trivialise, rather than enlighten. But since the mid-seventies there has been interest in more qualitative approaches, 'based on a conceptual framework which considers education in broad socio-cultural terms' (Stubbs and Delamont, 1976). This has led to a more eclectic research style and it looks as if classrooms will again be an academic growth area:

> The technology of schooling has not been conceptualised. Until this conceptualisation is satisfactorily done and the parameters and their functional relationships specified, we must necessarily remain at a primitive stage of analysis ... A formulation of the technology of teaching which includes instructional and managerial components is the sort of conceptual linkage needed to establish the connection between the production function and classroom instructional research traditions. (Bidwell, 1977, quoted in Westbury, 1979)

An English book (Bennett and McNamara, 1980) makes it clear that 'conceptualisation' has reached these shores: the aim is to develop a technology of 'teacher craft' and establish an area of 'professional studies as an academically rigorous, practically useful and scientifically productive activity'. Spooner (1980), writing as head of a large comprehensive school, offers a pertinent comment on this particular attempt to 'unweave rainbows' and reduce teaching to instructional and managerial concepts:

> Teachers ... rightly consider that what can be counted doesn't count ... Few teachers believe that recorded observations, particularly if limited to interaction analysis, will tell them anything of value they don't already know ... Fortunately there are rich elements in our heritage that should protect us from the worst excesses of educational research.

Yet teachers, like other folk, can easily be blinded by science and can accept the superficial results of this kind of research as potent insights. There is a real danger that the results of 'conceptualisation' will be incorporated into teacher education programmes, and guarantee a further diet of boring irrelevancies. Despite the superficialities of Bennett's research into primary schools (1976), it was widely interpreted as proof that traditional teaching methods worked better.

The fact is that analytical research of this kind is quite inappropriate for its subject matter. It attempts to do for teaching and classroom interaction what the research of Masters and Johnson has done for sexual interaction — to describe complex intellectual and emotional activity in terms of observed states and the alien language of physical science. It misses the whole point that what is going on is going on in the head — not in the laboratory. The results are of little general value, except to other researchers, anxious to spin the same elaborate webs. When we learn that scientists have produced a mathematical account of why a cricket ball spins, we smile indulgently, rightly concluding that it will make no difference whatever to the art of bowling: the process is too complex to make such exercises of more than academic value. Yet when the apparatus of psychologists and sociologists is harnessed to do its de-mythologising work on the infinitely more complex field of human interaction, we take it seriously and assume it will generate new truths. Certainly we can profit from shrewd and sensitive accounts of what goes on in classrooms: case study work can be of great value here. But attempts to establish a technology of the classroom are a quite different matter and one which will not help our understanding of what happens in them.

Self Evaluation in a School: a Case Study

In order to gain a better idea of what a formal self evaluation in a school would be like, and of the effects it might have, I took advantage in 1979–80 of an invitation from the head of a school to observe such an exercise. The school was one of two comprehensives serving a market town in East Anglia. It was purpose-built as a mixed eleven to eighteen comprehensive in phases, opening with 140 first-year pupils in 1971. The other school, a former grammar school, was reorganised at the same time and serves the more middle-class area of the town. After serious overcrowding in the mid-seventies, buildings are now almost complete: there are 72 staff, 1140 pupils on roll and 64 of these are in the sixth form.

The curriculum structure is fairly conventional. There are thirty-five periods of forty minutes weekly, and in years four and five the usual core-plus-option scheme prevails. The core subjects are English, mathematics, physical education, and a 'common course' including leisure activities, careers education and community education. From 1980-81 the core will no longer be divided into two ability bands, and will be extended to include design, humanities and science with a choice of subject within each of these areas. In the first three years all groups are full-range mixed-ability, except for separate remedial groups in French (taken by all pupils) in years two and three, and in science in year three where there is also ability setting for mathematics. In the first year all pupils take an integrated humanities course linking English, geography, history, drama and religious education. In the second year this continues, but without English and drama which become separate subjects. In the third year all subjects are taught separately.

The ethos of the school has three important aspects which are explicitly acknowledged by the head and staff. First, it is 'non-authoritarian': there is no uniform, nor are there prizegivings, staff gowns, prefects or headmaster's assemblies. Second, staff-pupil relationships are good: pupils like the school, there is little vandalism, and staff give generously of their time in working for pupils and talking about them. Third, the school takes seriously its responsibility for community education, with a vigorous parent-teacher association and an extensive programme of youth work and adult education.

Few staff are much over the age of forty, and there are many in their twenties and thirties. A visitor immediately picks up the atmosphere of informal dedication. The teachers are friendly, thoughtful, open-minded and articulate: the pupils move around purposefully and quietly but in a relaxed fashion. There is an unaggressive assurance about the place, and it is probably a measure of this confidence in what they are doing that the head and staff decided, in autumn 1979, to evaluate themselves. The self assessment had four declared objects:

1 To establish the aims and objectives of the school and its component departments.

2 To record present practice and achievement in all areas;

3 To evaluate the degree to which present practice and recent achievement fulfil the aims and objectives.

4 To identify needs for future development.

The assessment was completed during the autumn term, and the head's report was published to staff and governors in the following term. The core of the exercise was a self evaluation questionnaire to be completed by staff and submitted to the immediate head of the department or year group. Each immediate head, after discussion with his or her staff, submitted his own assessment to one of the deputy heads, depending on his role as academic, pastoral or organisational. Each deputy head then submitted his own consolidated assessment to the head, who used these assessments and his own self assessment to compile his final report. In this three-stage arrangement, the confidentiality of staff assessments was assured by limiting their access to each teacher's immediate head. The chairman of governors agreed to monitor the progress of the assessment, and a lecturer from a local college of education agreed to act as an external assessor, looking at the work of the head and of the school as a whole. A further provision of the original assessment schedule was for cross assessment: an independent assessment of each area of work was to be made by the head of another area not normally connected with that area. In the event, the self assessment process took up so much time that the cross assessment stage had to be abandoned.

My own involvement arose from the fact that the head and I had known each other for some years, and I had lectured at the school's in-service day in 1978. My request to follow the progress of the self assessment as part of a research project, by talking to staff about their perceptions of it, was readily granted. I spent three separate days in the school to this end, in each of the three terms in the academic year 1979-80 during which the assessment took place, the report appeared and the dust settled. On each occassion the staff I talked to had agreed to do so after prior approach by the first deputy: he took account of who happened to be free in each period, and tried to offer me a variety of backgrounds and attitudes. I relied entirely on his judgment in this. I made notes (but no recordings) of each talk and prepared a general summary of what I had heard immediately afterwards. Since my aim is to give an idea of what happens when teachers evaluate themselves, I shall draw on these three summaries to indicate the range of reactions and interpretations which were put to me.

Visit 14 September 1979

The assessment programme was viewed in different ways by different staff. None was distressed by it, but none had had time to reflect on its implications. Some thought it might achieve much; others had doubts about the very idea of assessment, or thought that for one reason or another it might not come to much in the end. All staff I spoke to saw its main value in terms of its benefit to the school as an internal process and document rather than an aid to understanding the school for parents or other members of its external community. Indeed, most saw dangers in making the final report too freely available. If it were to be of any value, it would need to refer to things that were bad or disappointing, as well as those that were good; but these could be taken out of context and misinterpreted.

It was thought that much depended on the way the personal self assessments were completed. Frankness and honesty were seen as virtues, but it might not be easy to exercise them. 'I suppose you tend to make the garden look rosy. You tend to look for the good rather than the bad.' Another took the view that 'abject self-criticism' was not required in completing the form; 'let them relate to what they're doing'. The purpose was 'to promote reflection, rather than action'.

(At this point, it is worth listing the questions on the individual assessment form. These, and the plan of the entire exercise, had of course been agreed by staff:

1 List your main job responsibilities within this area. How successful have you been? Consider your achievements against the targets and objectives.

2 What stands out in your mind as your best achievement?

3 Have you encountered any difficulties in your work? What are the reasons?

4 In what ways do you feel you need to improve in your job?

5 What parts of your job have interested you most? Interested you least?

6 What sort of work would you like to be doing in the future in this school? In your professional career?

7 Are there any problems you would like to discuss?)

No one was sure how much would come out of the self assessment as written output, but there was a feeling that the process of self assessment would be more valuable than its product in terms of these outputs. It was seen as a helpful way of making staff more aware of themselves and their links with other staff — as a form of sensitivity material.

The notion of evaluation came in for criticism, in that 'any kind of assessment can end up as a functionalist approach. The task is so huge — who can do the job thoroughly?' It might be a job for specialists; perhaps by HMI 'who both judge and recommend'. The stress here was on the humanity of teaching and the way it can conflict with conventional forms of assessment. It was doubted, though, whether LEA advisers would be free from bias, or competent even. And 'LEAs are interested in economy, not education'. It did not follow, though, that teachers were the best qualified to assess: 'Who the hell is a teacher to decide how good a school is?'

The time factor bulked large in teachers' minds. One estimate was that the exercise would cost all staff at least 'four to five hours, or one evening a week' and some much more. So it could not be accepted as a regular, annual event. 'Perhaps one in five years' was suggested by two different respondents. No one seemed enthusiastic about the idea of using a team of peers, CNAA-style, to make an independent, perhaps complementary, assessment. Neither, though, was there outright opposition. One mentioned the time factor, and failed to see how staff in working schools could be found with time to spare for membership of an evaluation team.

How far would the assessment programme promote curriculum change? Most agreed that there was a danger of complacency; the expectation was that the result of the exercise would be generally favourable, and so staff might be inclined to accept the present state. But 'the exercise could lead to greater cooperation among staff,' and 'it does make us focus on what we're doing'. Another said: 'Teaching is easy to do badly. What you do doesn't come back to haunt you. It's easy not to think about what you do. The job is very bitty.'

Most respondents raised the issue of how secure their completed assessments would be. If staff more senior than their immediate chiefs were to see them, this would be a constraint. But if their chiefs were to depersonalise the input statements in writing their reports, might they not take the opportunity to eliminate criticism of themselves? Self-study exercises raise a number of complex issues which are not easily seen at the beginning. One said he 'hadn't thought very hard about the implications of the whole thing.' Another pointed out that 'the ethos of the school fosters a spirit of self-criticsm', which could only be helpful.

Visit 28 March 1980

The general feeling was favourable — it was worth doing it. 'The most important thing is the process. The business of self-examination. Teachers lack self-confidence in evaluating what they're engaged in. It's helpful to suggest they're capable of assessing themselves and their colleagues'. Another said: 'A greater degree of awareness has come from filling up the questionnaire. When you write you focus attention, and crystallise'. For another, the assessment 'had lent definition to roles which were maybe a little vague'. Another said: 'The process is valuable — the end product a bit disappointing'. 'What was important was stating the aims and objectives of the school before we started. I understood them anyway, but my probationer found it useful'.

There was some criticism of the pyramidal way in which the assessment worked, with the questionaires being distilled at separate levels in the hierarchy. There's no doubt this scheme satisfied fears staff had, at the beginning, about confidentiality and the use to which their assessments might be put. But many now felt these fears had been exaggerated. 'I would have like to be able to read other people's assessments — it helps to see different emphasis and opinions. I'd hoped the assessment would mean we'd learn more about ourselves. Even though the channels are open here, it's hard to feel your views came through.' Most regretted there was not time to carry out the cross assessments. Had the exercise promoted more interaction between staff? 'Yes, the shape of the exercises led to that.' But another felt 'it probably hasn't made people more aware of other areas of the school. People tend to be too isolated'. Another thought that 'we've always been good at interaction. We've had a nice family atmosphere. No major changes have come out of the assessments, but we've written down bad points about present practice'. Another thought the assessment process 'hasn't yet made people more aware of each other in departments. There's still a big divide between the top staff and those lower down who argue "the others are paid to do it". The assessment hasn't changed that'. There was a difference of opinion about the form of the questionnaire: one thought 'it should have been more structured', while another said 'less structured questioning would have helped expose the human relations.'

On the specific issue of how far the assessment would lead to change, one remarked that 'this was not the point of the exercise'. Another, though, thought that as a result of the assessment 'we must spend a lot more time asking ourselves serious questions about what we're doing and why. We need a more systematic view. We have lived from hand to mouth, we have leapt at ideas without knowing why. There's a tendency to make decisions for next term. We're in a long-term business but we're making decisions in the short term. We need to ask, what are our curriculum plans, post 1985?' Another thought the assessment would 'probably not' lead to curriculum change, and added, 'This may not be the best way to promote change'. This was echoed by another, who thought the assessment was 'not meant to be a device for major change. We wouldn't want this. It's rather a way of improving the existing system. The basic philosophy of what we're doing should stay'.

At the beginning of the exercise, 'a tremendous defensiveness' was noted: 'maybe a deep underlying fear. It wasn't the probationers who voiced anxieties'. Another said that the honesty of the assessments was 'to some extent, a way of proving our integrity to each other'. Another, too, was struck by the honesty with which he found he could complete the self assessment, but added that 'in a school where there is less openness and trust, I would have been much less honest'. This is an interesting comment, since it suggests that a school's self assessment must perforce reflect its own value system. In this case, it was carried out in a school with outstandingly good relations among staff, and between staff and pupils. But perhaps a school will give itself the assessment it deserves: it seems likely that a school with a suspicious, authoritarian stance will uncover very little and be confirmed in its chosen path.

The real value of this particular self assessment will perhaps emerge from the follow up. One teacher asked, 'But what was the assessment for? To isolate problems? To make the machine run more smoothly? To get a picture of the life of the school?'To some extent, no doubt, all of these things; my impression is that most staff saw the exercise as a study of things as they are, rather than of what they might become. Several staff said that they would like to think procedures of this kind would become part of teacher professionalism. The key question, I think, is: how far is the self-assessment questionnaire a helpful device to promote this? The danger is that it locks the teacher's thinking too closely to the current scene. The critical link is that between self assessment and curriculum change, and in some schools the former could become a substitute for the latter. As one teacher said, 'self assessment would be more difficult in a school that lacked commitment. Down-at-heel schools are hardly likely to benefit from it. In some schools deputies have gone round with clipboards as if they were inspectors.'

Visit 26 June 1980

This visit was made at a time when not much of the summer term
was left, and the memory of the self-assessment was not as fresh as
the term before. The governors had received the head's report on the
self assessment exercise, and this had also been given to staff. I sensed
that expectations regarding the outcome of the internal review were
somewhat dimmed: 'When the head's report was published, many
thought that what they'd said hadn't come through. The report was
very stimulating and interesting, but I felt it brushed aside some key
points. People had made comments and expected something to be
done about it. So it looked like a whitewash job. The assessment does
need to be followed up'. Another said: 'I felt the report didn't say
enough — little bits in isolation. There was a lack of positive feedback. The response was rather generalised. I felt it would all lead to
far-reaching changes like vertical grouping or block timetabling. It
would be a pity to let it lie, although that feeling is around'.

Another teacher could barely remember completing the questionnaire. He was sceptical about the value of the exercise: 'People are
very concerned about audience, about for whom they're writing. People's answers might well be mediated by a concern about who was
reading them. My feeling about the whole thing is that schools and
teachers are very inward looking — people don't like you looking into
their classrooms. The exercise didn't break down that kind of
reserve. The feeling that the teacher in the classroom likes to be boss
is the sticking point of the whole exercise. Institutions are good at
covering their tracks. I wonder how much change will result'.
Another respondent made some similar points: 'Staff self
assessment? People were suspicious. They became over-optimistic
about the results — they thought that all the things they didn't like
would be changed. This hasn't happened, and so I'd say it's been a
disappointment for most people ... In the short term, you sit down to
write your assessment and say — I haven't coped with that. But that
may not change the way you teach'.

For some, though, the value of the self assessment exercise was appreciated: 'The questionnaire forced me to look into areas where I
hadn't performed well, and made me ask why ... It got people talking
again in the staffroom. It's partly geographical. The upper/lower
school split separates us. The split isn't a good idea. We need a
building in the middle ... People ought to look at themselves every
year, and people ought to get praise and blame ... It's a funny thing
about this school: everyone is struck by how unconventional the

school is, but the teaching is very ordinary really'. Another said: 'I see self-examination as part of my professional role, anyway'. And another: 'It made you think about what you're doing. Everything normally goes so quickly. Also, you think of your subject through the eyes of the school.

Would the self assessment lead to much curriculum change? 'Self assessment in many schools will just be reassurance. Here, we do need to look at the curriculum. And if we do it, it will be only partly because of our own internal assessment. We all see that self assessment must be part of what a teacher does. But it must arise from the curriculum discussion and deliberation which we now need to see going on here'.

During the morning's interviews, it became clear that a number of teachers were making the point that they did reflect on their work in the normal course of things, but not necessarily in occasions like departmental meetings: more commonly these insights would occur casually. I pursued the idea that this kind of reflective activity might need some sort of formalising structure, of which the self assessment exercise was one possibility. Could other forms be devised which might make such activity a more natural part of a teacher's professional work? 'The ideas about my professional work come out piecemeal and need to be brought together. Yes — some sort of formal process might be useful. But when you do institutionalise it, it becomes less free. I don't like this isolation of departments'. I suggested that a device like asking an English teacher into a mathematics department meeting to ask leading questions about mathematics policy might be helpful. This was thought to be 'a good idea ... That would be incredibly useful ...Yes, I like very much the idea of using teachers as educator/change agents in that way'.

Another teacher, who taken a PGCE (Post Graduate Certificate of Education) course after working in industry, was critical of self assessment, and also of classroom interaction studies as a way of developing professional self-awareness: 'It's very simplistic stuff. I saw it in my university department. You want to know so much more about it. I don't see how you can transfer it to your own experience. We had a series of seminars, called "situations" — watching films, discussing incidents. It's a nonsense — they're not derived from your own experience. You can discuss these dimensions endlessly — but it offers nothing to classroom practice'. I tried out my suggestion of using in department meetings a teacher from another specialism prepared to adopt the educator/change agent role: 'One would hope to be in a department where the reflection and interaction you mention go on informally. You're right, though — one needs a formalisation — the idea of the outsider could work. The boundaries are clearly defined — there wouldn't be any animus. It might be that teachers in a school could do that. You're asking for a kind of intelligence'.

It was interesting to discover that an able and thoughtful teacher of English, who mentioned that he didn't like language testing, was unaware that the Bullock committee had called for monitoring. Another said: 'In our department there's a move to get back to streaming. There's a feeling we're not doing the best for children. We need more preparation and training for mixed ability. I don't organise the class into groups. I don't know how to do it'.

I was left with the impression that self-study schemes may easily be thought to promise more than they can deliver. They need careful planning, and probably advice from independent agents should be available throughout the process. Bringing in LEA advisers as part of it might well be helpful; the result might be much more valuable than deploying them for formal inspections. But this would presuppose a different approach to the advisory role than seems to have been exhibited towards this school.

Evaluation and Curriculum Action

The above notes indicate a variety of staff responses to a school-based self evaluation. Teachers were invited to review their work in the light of the school's declared intentions. The emphasis was on procedures and on process, and the chosen form of the exercise encouraged staff to reflect on the way they set about their work. It was an internal evaluation, concentrating on transactions rather than output measures, and its purpose was not merely to assess things as they are, but also to make value judgments about actions and 'identify needs for future development' — to determine the extent and direction of change. It was an enterprising step to take, and a difficult one to judge.

The programme absorbed much time and energy, and the style of evaluation might not be to the taste of schools with a more formal pattern of relationships. This was a school where the staff got on easily with each other, shared a number of implicit assumptions about schooling and where authority rested on performance rather than status. Even so, at least one teacher felt the evaluation 'didn't break down that kind of reserve' — didn't reveal the fine grain of classroom life. It may be that greater self-revelation would result from adopting a more elaborate, more 'responsive' style of evaluation of the sort referred to in the previous section, and perhaps using an internal or external specialist evaluator to apply structure to the interactions between staff. But at least the school went beyond a mere list of output measures — as discussed in an earlier section — and made the attempt to get staff to evaluate themselves. It would, in any event, be folly to try to evaluate such a self evaluation. In the short term, my summaries of staff comments might, or might not, be suggestive. In the long term, it is always difficult to ascribe a particular outcome to a particular cause. Historical judgment is problematic, too.

What I think is necessary, though, is a closer look at the nature of evaluation and a critical look at the claims made for it. I have noted that these claims are of two kinds. For those of a technocratic, managerial cast of mind, evaluation is a way of establishing whether 'targets' have been hit, as part of some organised process in which ends can be clearly defined, and separated from the appropriate means. The aim is 'effective decision making', and evaluation is essentially a matter of technique: 'The latent assumption ... is that the chances of learning occurring in line with those staff objectives are greater where the objectives are explicit and where the degree to which they are attained is regularly evaluated' (Shipman, 1979). The tendency here is to look for *output* measures, if possible of a numerical kind, and if the evaluation is *internal* the stress will be on pupil records and profiles, marks and grades, checklists and statistical data. If *external*, monitoring will take the form of tests of pupil performance and a formal analysis of school aims and procedures. Key words are objective, systematic, methodical, effective.

The other justification for evaluation seems to spring from what Oakeshott (1962) termed 'modern Rationalism': the belief that reason alone can determine 'the worth of a thing, the truth of a opinion or the propriety of an action'. By dissecting an activity into components, it must ultimately be possible to explain, and so express the activity as a formal process. Thus the emphasis is not on the output but on the *transactions* which compose the activity. There is less concern with technique, and more with values: it is recognised that judgements must be made, but subjectivity does not make evaluation impossible — simply more difficult:

> Evaluations always depend upon values, either explicit or implicit, and there is much to be said for making as explicit as possible the underlying value judgments. The very act of, and attempt at, evaluation may clarify our thoughts. Consideration of aims and objectives, and the development of guidelines and frameworks for the curriculum, are

sharpened, not only by a consideration of the underlying values, but also by the attempt at evaluation. (Straughan and Wrigley, 1980)

Evaluation of this kind, whether internal or external, will treat numerical data with caution, and instead rely on observations in a local context; it will set out different perspectives, different professional judgments. It may, or may not, attempt to make its own judgments. Key words are subjective, responsive, negotiated, transactional.

This latter style appeals particularly to academics and is often seen as sharply divided from the former: the 'productivity' model is despised by those who want evaluation to be 'illuminative'. Yet outside the pages of learned journals there can be a considerable blurring between the two types. Eisner (1979) points out that

> To emphasise, as I have just done, the distinctive characteristics of qualitative inquiry is not to suggest that those who use such methods reject quantitative procedures. They do not. What they do reject is the assumption that objectivity can only be secured through quantitative or scientific methods.

Fair enough: yet while some new styles of classroom research appear to spring from a more interpretive, less quantitative approach to the business, their aim of developing a new technology of teaching indicates an affinity with scientific forms of inquiry. And an emphasis on stating aims and objectives may, as in the above examples, be common to both approaches to evaluation.

My own sympathies lie with the kind of position adopted by Eisner. And skilful case studies of school processes along these lines should offer useful illumination of educational practice and decision-making. But it seems to me to be a further, and much more contentious, step to argue that inquiry of this kind (or, of course, of a more quantitative, output-centred kind) should become both an essential part of professional practice, and be seen as the essential preliminary to curriculum innovation.

Whatever style of evaluation is adopted, evaluation itself has two indisputable aspects: it can only consider what has already happened, and it can only exist as a formal activity — the thing that 'evaluators' do — as a separate activity from what has happened. Even if the evaluator is 'self evaluating' by consciously reflecting on his action, evaluation is an activity separate from the action. Whatever the technique or style of self evaluation or classroom monitoring that is being advocated, all have in common a retrospective look at a past activity, separated from that activity so that the self-consciousness of the teacher-evaluator may be heightened.

I want to argue that this view of evaluation (and of self evaluation) misconceives the nature of the action of teaching and of curriculum activity in general, and is therefore at the least irrelevant, and potentially both confusing and destructive. For the activity of teaching, like that of the scientist, the painter, the politician, the cook, is conducted within the existing 'idiom of the activity' (Oakeshott, 1962). And we learn how to do it not from analytical rules, but from the practical pursuit of the activity itself:

> Gradually ... we improve and extend our first knowledge of how to pursue the activity. Among such means ... is the analysis of the activity, the definition of the rules and principles which seem to inhere in it and in reflection upon these rules and principles. But these rules and principles are mere abridgments of the activity itself; they do not exist in advance of the activity, they cannot properly be said to govern it and they cannot provide the impetus of the activity. A complete mastery of these principles may exist alongside a complete inability to pursue the activity to which they refer. For the pursuit of the activity does not consist in the application of these principles; and even if it did, the knowledge of how to apply them (the knowledge actually involved in pursuing the activity) is not given in a knowledge of them. (Oakeshott, 1962)

Teaching depends on *practical knowledge*, and so does curriculum development. And practical knowledge 'can neither be taught nor learned, but only imparted and acquired'. Certainly one can sometimes associate a practical activity with *technical knowledge* — 'rules, principles, directions, maxims'. This is propositional knowledge — 'knowing that' — and it can be written down in books and papers. But learning these 'is never more than the meanest part of education in an activity' — what matters is the practical knowledge — 'knowing how' — without which we cannot be said to be capable of the activity. In deriving technical knowledge, the methods of science may be appropriate; but the scientist also needs practical knowledge in order to practise the activity of science, and it is a gross error to imagine that science can offer a total description of an activity. We can only practise an activity, and make judgments about the activity, within the practical idiom of the activity.

For example, the writer of a textbook on musical counterpoint (the practical knowledge of writing melodies according to fixed rules) advises:

> To point out a greater or lesser degree of contrapuntal quality in a piece of music is not to evaluate its success as music ... However com-

plex the problem, (the student) should not take satisfaction in its solution unless the result is of high standards as pure music. The real test
is how it sounds. (Piston, 1970)

One cannot evaluate a curriculum action in terms of its 'contrapuntal
quality' — how far it accords with established rules and checklists,
pre-determined objectives and concepts: what matters is 'how it
sounds', the practice of the action.

Those who advocate a technocratic style of evaluation are seeking
to analyse curriculum activity in order to define rules and principles,
aims and objectives. But, as Oakeshott argues, these cannot exist in
advance of the activity. Hence the absurdity of a handbook for 'self
assessment for secondary schools' which declares:

> The process of self evaluation can only be meaningful if the proposals
> or plans that emerge fit defined aims and objectives. It follows
> therefore, that a school must be clear as to what are its aims and objec-
> tives.

Assuredly, there must be a set of agreed broad aims — a rationale of
the school's curriculum: but to claim that this must be expressed as a
set of detailed objectives is to misconceive the nature and value of
aims, and of the activity of education itself.

Furthermore, any defined principles cannot describe or adequately
govern the activity, nor can they 'provide the impetus of the activity'.
To suggest, therefore, that evaluation should proceed in advance of
curriculum change is to misunderstand the nature of a practical activity. Evaluation as a formal, separate analysis based on past performance of the activity — whether 'psychometric' or 'responsive', and
however sensitive to context or democratic principles — can only
throw a flickering light on the technical knowledge we acquire of the
activity. Certainly it cannot govern the activity or determine new
ways of carrying out the activity within its idiom. Even if we could
determine rules and principles by analysis and evaluation, the activity
does not (as those adhering to the 'technocratic paradigm' believe)
consist in applying these principles. Neither can the knowledge of
how the activity is pursued — sought after by those adhering to the
'interpretive paradigm' — give us knowledge of the activity itself.

There are further dangers in self evaluation. For the successful
practice of curriculum activity depends upon our acquiring practical
knowledge — the artistry, style and insight which gives distinction to
the activity — and making it our own: making it instinctive, almost
involuntary, so that we can take technique for granted and deploy intuitive judgement. The risk in studied self evaluation is that 'self-

consciousness is asked to be creative, and habit is given the role of critic; what should be subordinate has come to rule, and its rule is misrule' (Oakeshott, 1980). Again, I would offer an example from another activity which, like teaching, is dependent on creative judgement. In writing of the craft of the novel, Colin Wilson (1975) stresses the need to take its rules for granted — 'something the writer picks up as he goes along' — and so become free to explore a creative passion:

> The central problem of human consciousness is connected with the 'robot', the mechanical part of us. As highly complex beings, we need to be able to do a great many things mechanically, from breathing to driving the car and talking foreign languages. In fact, our 'robot' does most difficult things far better than we can do them 'deliberately' ... If I tried to think about my fingers as I typed, I would do it badly again.

It is interesting that Stibbs (1979) uses a similar analogy, writing of the need for teachers not to be too rule-bound and intolerant in helping pupils acquire complex skills:

> A learner of a language, native or foreign, may be thrown by being asked to read aloud a text that he is beginning to make sense of through reading silently. It is like asking a pianist to think about his fingers.

A pianist gets better at sight reading — at continuously solving new problems — not by listening to tape recordings, or self-consciously thinking about his technical conformity to sets of rules. He gets better by doing it — providing he has the capacity to absorb the idiom of the activity by thinking about this practical activity while he is doing it. But the thinking is not distinct from the action. This will be true of the carpenter, the cook, the teacher, and, as Ryle (1972) pointed out, of the tennis player: 'His using his wits and his playing the game are a single operation, not two rival (or even allied) occupations.'

Those who would make evaluation a separate, formal activity, or — as in 'self evaluation' — a conscious conceptualisation of the observable aspects of an action, are failing to recognise this unity, and wrongly supposing that an intelligent action must be preceded by ratiocination, and that the only access to knowledge is through theory and propositional knowledge. The talents of skilful practitioners might, indeed, be undermined by the intrusions of 'self evaluation', in that the unity of thought and action is broken by self-consciously separating out the 'robot' part of the activity — the ability to solve practical problems which has become intuitive. For those who are to be trained to become practitioners, the implication is that lectures on learning theory, and on the supposed technical knowledge of rules and maxims, will merely obstruct the essential process, which is to acquire the idiom of the activity by being allowed to do it while in contact with those who are practising it. Claxton (1980) notes that a book on tennis describes how people can learn to play tennis quickly and easily by not trying:

> Not trying to hit the ball 'right' ... not 'correct' their grip, stance or aim, but simply allowing the body to move in its own way and noticing what happens. The noticing is not in order to do it better: accurate noticing is sufficient for a doing-it-better to emerge spontaneously. The same process can work in learning to teach, if the learners can surrender to the transitional state of experimenting, being wrong, and (worst of all) being seen to be wrong.

Permeating schools, teachers and training institutions with the notion of evaluation, and the need to reflect self-consciously on action, makes it that much harder to make a mistake: much harder to realise that learning is a much more natural process than one would ever believe from the outpourings of learning theorists and classroom researchers. Self criticism, and too overt a tradition of criticism, can also bring other problems in its wake. A Russian book (Kaidalov and Suimenko, 1979) examines this well-established Soviet practice, and notes how readily it can be abused in order to settle personal scores, or enhance one's own prestige: 'Utterly undistinguished people, who are mediocre in their everyday work, will all of a sudden display an uncommon zeal at meetings ... Having come to the notice of management ... they begin to get elected to various commissions'. These comments are all the more telling, since they are published within a society where a commitment to self criticism is part of the Rationalism (in Oakeshott's usage) which underlies the political basis of that society.

The fundamental error in all this is that of exalting evaluation into a separate activity. By labelling the way in which we appraise our actions and lifting it out of context, we attack the very basis on which the successful completion of an action depends: we misconceive the nature of change as a part of action, and the evaluative effect of our intentions upon the action:

> To act is to act on something and so to change it. The something that is acted on and that becomes changed by the action is a state of affairs in the world. In human action the change is brought about by the agency of a person who is also an observer. The agent therefore has

beliefs about the situation in which and on which he is acting. He also has intentions about the way in which that situation is to be changed by his action. (Langford, 1972)

Those who would make evaluation a separate activity and an explicit part of professionalism have failed to note that the person who acts is himself an observer, with beliefs and intentions about the effects of his action. If, therefore, we seek to promote curriculum change and appropriate styles of action, the essential starting point must be a discussion of beliefs and intentions: 'Practical reasoning proceeds from *our* intentions which are evident from acting purposefully' (Langford, 1973). The critical aspect of curriculum development is not, and cannot be, evaluation or self evaluation: it must deal with prior intentions, attitudes and assumptions, with the conflicting value judgments which are implicit in the arts of practical reasoning and deliberation. And this is an activity which cannot be separated from the practical performance of curriculum action.

The evaluators also exalt the status of technical knowledge, which must always be an abridgment or reduction of curriculum activity, and which can in any event never become a part of the activity. The knowledge which really matters is practical knowledge, which cannot be made the subject of articles, papers, books, case studies or evaluation documents. A preoccupation with evaluation will not mean that teachers can profitably use evaluation: but it may well mean that evaluation uses them. And, at the end of the day, a teacher may be perfectly skilled in the techniques of self evaluation, and yet still be an inadequate teacher.

6 Accountability, Evaluation and Curriculum Change

Evaluation always implies judgment. Like every action, it expresses an intention and the intention of an evaluation is to look at the past with a view to the future. For we cannot look at the past without making judgments about what we choose to see, and how we see it: and these judgments will reflect a value position which will be served by the act of evaluating. Thus it is not possible, as the APU at first argued, to see assessment as a neutral activity, like taking an aerial photograph. Indeed, a photograph will always be taken to serve some intention, unless it is a casual act. During the 1939–45 war, the British derived much information from aerial photographs of Germany, and developed cameras to produce what they were looking for. At the end of the war, the RAF specialists in photographic intelligence were able to examine the corresponding work done in Germany, and found that the Germans had taken beautiful photographs, but with not real understanding of how they could be used: 'The Germans seemed to have thought that because a camera is a machine all you've got to do is improve mechanical quality' (Babington Smith, 1961). The intention will always determine the form of an evaluation.

The intention will also embody some judgment about the use of the evaluation, although this may not be explicit, and the data produced by an evaluation may always be used in some unintended and possibly misleading way. Thus a student's A-level GCE grades may be used to determine his acceptance by a medical school, although these grades are known to be a poor predictor of success in higher education, and would appear to have no specific connection with the qualities required by a doctor. The APU tests may be conceived as criterion referenced, but they are already being used to define norms of performance. The APU science team may not wish their tests to influence the curriculum, but the first school science textbook based on their conceptual analysis has now been published, in advance even of the results of the first APU science tests.

The intended future result of an evaluation may simply be to preserve the status quo: aims and objectives may have been specified, and the evaluation may be to determine deviations from these norms and allow corrective action to be taken. Usually, though, it is at least implicit that the evaluation might produce data which would influence these norms, and most writers on evaluation see evaluation as a direct means of achieving change: 'The main purpose of curriculum evaluation is the improvement of teaching in classrooms' (Elliott, 1979a). Even when our evaluation is simply confined to administering a test to a pupil, we use these data on what has already happened to determine some future course of action. If it is a diagnostic test, we decide on what to teach next: if it is an intelligence test, we decide whether to give him the job or not. And in choosing such a test to make such a decision, we make assumptions about the job and judge how to assess aptitude for it. The act of evaluation always implies value judgments about a past event and always implies value judgments about future events.

Evaluation is therefore an activity fraught with danger, since if we are looking at things in an inadequate way (as were the Germans at their aerial photographs) we shall produce inadequate or misleading data. And in any case, once such data are public we cannot control the use made of them, whether they are adequate data or not. Finally, the link between evaluation and improvement looks beguiling, but the absence of an explicit logical connection means that if change arises, it may not be what was intended.

In this final chapter I shall look at the substantial weight of responsibility which educational evaluation seems increasingly to be carrying. There is the use of evaluation to render schools and teachers accountable; its use to decide on the aptness of curriculum innovation; its use in school examinations to decide children's futures; and its advocacy by academics as an element of professionalism and a device for promoting curriculum change. Such evaluation rests on some formal assessment of an action, separate from its performance and based only on external evidence for it. How well are assessment procedures fitted for the tasks of evaluation? Is evaluation inevitable?

Accountability

The notion that schools should be able to account for their actions is hardly new. A head teacher knows he may be called upon to render an account to the school's governors; the LEA's officers, members or advisers; a visiting HMI; the school parent-teacher association; to other teachers on some representative school body; possibly to pupils, if a school council or forum exists; and to individual parents. Traditionally, responsibility for education in England and Wales has been diffused through the layers of the administrative system, and accountability procedures have been implicit in the main. Furthermore, the complexity of educational decisions has been recognised by devolving considerable authority on to the head of a school, and this pattern was established in the last century.

During the 1970s education began to look increasingly costly as the economic climate took a turn for the worse, and the feeling grew that schools could do better. The notion of more explicit forms of accountability was imported from North America, and enshrined in the text of the Callaghan government's Green Paper on education (1977):

> Growing recognition of the need for schools to demonstrate their accountability to the society which they serve requires a coherent and soundly based means of assessment for the educational system as a whole, for schools and for individual pupils.

It is also asserted that 'schools must have aims against which to judge the effectiveness of their work and hence the kind of improvements that they may need to make from time to time.' Accountability, then, is to be based on finite, formal assessment; schools, which exist to serve society rather than their pupils, are to derive these measures of assessment from formal aims; and the assessments are to be used to effect improvements. This is an instrumental, production model of schooling and accurately reflects the kind of thinking which has proved so unhelpful to American schools.

This is not the place for further analysis of the concept of accountability: Sockett (1980) gives a useful summary of the issues, remarking that 'the main point on which all its advocates would agree is that (accountability) is an attempt to *improve* the quality of education'. The means by which accountability is achieved is the device of evaluation, upon which the burden of improvement therefore falls. In previous chapters I have looked at the forms evaluation can take, and I shall now consider how far evaluation can form the basis of an accountability system.

External assessment through performance monitoring appeals to politicians, administrators, psychometricians and even some teachers, but it interferes with the process it attempts to measure and can only be based on a gross abridgement of that process. Further, as Wilson (1972) points out, we cannot be sure that the result of testing X is a measure of 'what went on in X's head', nor that it was the *cause* of the observed behaviour. Tests, in short, do not measure what they purport to measure, and it is impossible to know for certain just what they do measure. A small shift of emphasis in a test can produce a big change in results. Wood (1977) gives a telling example of two mathematics questions taken from an O-level examination. The first states: In a class of pupils, the ratio of the number of boys to the number of girls is 2:3. The candidate is then asked to state the number of boys in the class, if x is the total number of pupils in the class, by selecting an answer from 5 possibilities. In the event, fifty-six per cent chose the correct answer of $2x/5$. Although an easy question on ratio, the answers suggest an insecure knowledge of it. But another question on ratio told candidates that £252 was to be divided in the ratio 5:6:7 between three people, and asked for the difference between the largest share and the smallest share. This time, eighty-five per cent of the candidates selected the right answer, £28. On this evidence, ratio is well understood by the majority of candidates. Wood points out that 'the level of response depends on the questions set', and the APU cannot be any more 'objective' about this than an examination board. There is no such thing as an objective test. And however explicit the aims and objectives of an educational programme, there can be no certainty that tests derived from those objectives actually test them.

Neither does it follow that evaluation will of itself improve quality. Erlandson (1973), referring to American experience, writes:

> In many quarters there seems to be an implicit faith that evaluation can, by itself, correct many evils in the schools. It is, apparently, assumed that if we know how badly we are doing we will be better off. This is not necessarily so, any more than it is true that a chest X-ray will, by itself, cure the tuberculosis it reveals ... So often evaluations of school programmes ... lead to no action at all.

So often the effect of mass data is to stun into inaction. One reads, for example, that the 1978 National Food Survey showed that 'meat and meat products contributed more than thirty per cent of the protein in the average household diet' (*Guardian*, 16 June 1980) and one wonders what use such information can possibly have outside government departments. The APU will pile up equally inert heaps of data, as will LEA surveys: and because education is a much more complex activity than eating, it will be infinitely harder to make sense of it. Again, the American experience is enlightening. Oregon is a state which took some trouble to avoid the worst excesses of accountability (its unofficial state motto is said to be, Don't californicate

Oregon) and was singled out for approval by Burstall and Kay (1978) on their APU-sponsored trip to the USA: 'The approach so far adopted by the APU is more closely related to the Oregon pattern than the others ... Such an approach, while it comes nearest to answering the questions society is asking about education, puts the maximum strain on assessment techniques and it remains to be seen how far these can be extended to fulfil the task.' An American study (National Education Association, 1978) throws some light on this:

> Oregon, for example, reports that since the pupil proficiency requirements have been enacted, Department of Public Instruction staff who provide technical assistance in assessment far outnumber staff who provide technical assistance in basic and general education. Assessment efforts have mushroomed to such an extent that it is difficult to pinpoint state costs for the various aspects of evaluation and testing.

It emerges that 'Michigan has spent so much time, effort and money over the past few years of attempting to implement their public school testing programme that the Governor has budgeted 250,000 dollars to evaluate the state's assessment programme'. Florida, with a commitment to student accountability through functional literacy tests, conducted a study (Florida Public School Districts, 1976) which reported 'strong indications that many students are over-tested ... almost no one really uses the data to effect changes or improvements in students' educational experiences ... No one is able to identify either short-term or long-range uses of state programme assessment data for policy makers'.

An English study of accountability (Becher et al., 1980) looks at a number of possible strategies, and can say little in favour of performance testing:

> The main limitation of testing, considered as a policy option, is its inability to throw any light on causes and effects. Test results assert, but never explain. If they show up an anomaly, the reasons for it have to be investigated separately ... In the context of accountability, a testing programme serves the modest but useful function of a warning light on an instrumental panel: it provides no substitute for the professional skills of maintenance and repair.

And there are, of course, much cheaper and less contentious warning systems to hand: more advisers, or a closer study of public examinations results even, are obvious possibilities.

The adverse effects of monitoring programmes by means of psychometric tests are now emerging from North America. For a detailed report by the US Commission on the Humanities (Lyman, *et al.* 1980) finds that English, history, foreign languages and the arts generally have lost ground in American schools over the last decade, and links this decline specifically with the growth of testing:

> Improving the reading and writing skills of students is a goal of and a foundation for study in the humanities. But wherever basic education concentrates exclusively on the three Rs or *whenever academic achievement is reduced to what can be measured by standardised testing*, the humanities are likely to be misunderstood as expendable frills. The notion that the humanities improve the mind, nurture the spirit, and inform moral and civic choices can be all but lost in the rush back to basics (my italics).

If we recall that NAEP, the American precursor of the APU, began work in 1967; that NAEP operates a far broader testing programme than the APU; and that the last decade has been a time of immense testing activity in the US, then this passage is both an indictment of mass monitoring, and a warning that the influence of the APU on British education may be even more dire than that of national and local testing on American education. The report concludes that 'A dramatic improvement in the quality of education in our elementary and secondary schools is the highest educational priority for America in the 1980s'. Nothing could more clearly demonstrate that a decade spent in the belief that assessment will lead to improvement is a decade of wasted effort and, indeed, of actual decline.

Nearer home, an investigation by a school psychologist (Rennie, 1980) has exposed the inadequacies of testing, even when used merely as a screening device. In 1973, all seven year olds in the former West Riding of Yorkshire were tested for vocabulary, reading and design copying, much as subsequently recommended in the 1975 Bullock Report and carried out in many LEAs. Six years later, these pupils (now thirteen year old) were checked against the earlier predictions. There were massive errors: the screening mistakenly identified many children as likely failures when they were not, and missed many others who subsequently needed special attention. Three out of every four who later needed help from the school psychological service were missed by the screening test. Yet LEA blanket testing of pupils for reading and mathematics is frequently justified as a screening device.

As a form of external evaluation, systems based on performance testing have the appeal of apparent objectivity. And standardised testing has the aura of a precise science about it. But the evidence suggests that tests should be used only with extreme caution, and cannot replace the sensitivity   and perception of the individual teacher. The only alternative approach to school accountability from outside is one based on some interpretive model of evaluation, which will recognise the subjectivity of its assessments from the start. Such methods cannot offer quick, numerical answers, and will be costly because human judgment is more expensive than machine-scored tests. They allow us to side-step the problems which arise when the methods of science are applied to educational processes, but difficulties remain. Becher (1978) mentions three. First, what of the preoccupations and prejudices brought to the study by the evaluator? Becher finds it impracticable to suppose 'that anyone's existing belief system can be suppressed, and absurd in its failure to draw on the skill and past experience of the evaluator'. Second, there is the argument that the evaluator must negotiate what he writes with those he evaluates: 'that the job of evaluation consists of trying to get everyone's agreeement to publish what they have said about others and what others have said about them.' This Becher regards as 'a piece of pie-in-the-sky', and certainly I find the idea of negotiating what one sees to be the case as a very curious one. Third, it is often argued that the evaluator should not judge, but simply offer evidence so that others can do the judging. I would agree with Becher that this is 'an abdication of a perfectly legitimate responsibility. An intelligent outsider ... will certainly at times be in a better position than any of the participants themselves to say of a particular practice that it seems pointless ...' But there is little agreement among illuminative evaluators on these issues, and it could be argued that such an evaluation will either end up telling us little we didn't know already, or (by the appropriate choice of evaluator) telling us what we want to hear.

It seems unlikely that a local authority committed to evaluation would readily abandon performance testing in favour of illuminative methods. Apart from the greater cost, it would be exchanging uncertainties for ambiguities. But if it is a matter of evaluating not a school system but a particular curriculum programme, one would hope that the funding authority would look for something more sophisticated than mere tests. Such an evaluation would not be confined to the declared aims and objectives, and would look at the context of the innovation and its unintended consequences. But the skill of the evaluator will be paramount; his judgment will be decisive. He can only interpret data, conduct interviews and hand out questionaires. They can all be done well, or badly: 'All types of interview data are subject to the possibility of distortion due to the context in which the data is [sic] being collected ... Wording of questions is quite definitely an art and there are few, if any, rules to guide the questionnaire designer' (Henderson, 1978).

Most so-called 'evaluations' of courses, conferences and the like are of uncertain value. But they appear to bring confidence and independence to a process which relies heavily on happenstance and arbitrary judgment. Although the cost of such an evaluation is often considerable, it may be accepted quite readily. Bureaucrats have, too, an insatiable appetite for data regardless of its quality or worth. Hence the role of the 'evaluator' is defined, and must be justified by some kind of printed output. But the truth is that there is absolutely no surefire, incontestable way of evaluating an educational activity.

Some, though, are better than others. In general the passage of time is a help in making all judgments of this kind, and this is one reason why longitudinal studies, like that carried out by Burstall (1974) on French in primary schools, seem to be more convincing. Yet these findings were not received without controversy, and are still not accepted wholly by many modern languages advisers. Just as evaluation is a political activity, so also will be the response of funding authorities to evaluation findings. Opportunities to save money are rarely passed up, particularly if — as in the primary French case — the project appeared to confirm what was already generally evident.

If our concern is to secure positive educational change by external evaluation, we are likely to be disappointed. The central difficulty is that, as I have argued, evaluation is integral to the activity of teaching or curriculum planning and cannot be separated. There is no substitute for a consideration of the input to the action, rather than its output. The particular danger with performance testing is that, far from leading to change, it will simply reinforce the emphasis schools already place on basic skills. It looks as if the DES has begun to realise that, in financing further forays by APU research teams into curriculum monitoring, they are seeking the unattainable. An October 1980 paper *The Work of Schools* states that 'Other areas of the curriculum which are being considered by the APU concern pupils' aesthetic and physical development, and technological understanding, but national monitoring in these areas will not necessarily follow'. The political contingency has been met by tests of English, mathematics and science, with foreign languages in the offing. But in educational terms this is a distressing and lop-sided outcome. Schools are encouraged to give still further weight to the 'basics', and the humanities are substantially ignored. The 'six lines of development' of Brian Kay, the APU's founder, have turned out to be a recipe for a grossly diminished curriculum. Yet Kay has, since leaving the APU and becoming chief inspector for teacher training, talked of 'the built-in conservatism of the teaching profession' and asked 'why curriculum reforms and innovations were being implemented so little' (*Guardian*, 20 June 1980). One very good reason will increasingly be the influence of the APU.

To summarise: external forms of school accountability will prove costly and contentious, and may lower teacher morale. They will generate data which may be very little used. They will foster an impoverished view of education and deskill the teacher at a time when his professional skills are more important than ever. They may cause curriculum innovation to stop, but are unlikely to make it start. They have absorbed the energies of many well-intentioned individuals, and will doubtless continue to do so. They can also prove extremely profitable to the would-be evaluators. But *au fond,* they are not to do with education: they are to do with saving money. Yet at the end of the day, there may be little to show for it all but a curtailed curriculum and a less resilient teaching force.

I turn next to internal forms of accountability. These are linked perforce to the professional activities of teachers, and at first sight are preferable. But the forms such accountability can take need to be considered carefully. I have argued that where accountability is fostered by LEAs through the devices of formal reports, lists of performance data and questionnaires tied to in-service courses, it is a covert way of reducing school autonomy and modifying the curriculum. It may be that the autonomy of the school should be reviewed, and that the curriculum should be re-shaped: I have elsewhere argued the case for both (Holt, 1979). But these are matters for public debate, and not for action by stealth, or by the reductionist device of the checklist.

It is worth remarking that accountability cuts both ways, and I am waiting to read of a head teachers' association which devises a checklist of questions for administrators to work through. 'When did you last spend a day in a school?' would make a good starting point; and education committee chairmen might ask the CEO, 'When did you last personally sit on the appointment committee for a head teacher?' I have had the good fortune to serve an authority whose CEO regarded this as the most important thing he was paid to do: yet it is surprising how often one hears that the appointment to even a secondary school headship has been made by deputies or chief advisers. There is a wealth of evidence and experience to confirm that the critical influence in a school is that of the head. The irony is that the same managerial enthusiasm which leads CEOs to devise accountability schemes keeps them so busy that they have little time to make educational judgements which might, just conceivably, improve things a little.

Two other approaches to internal accountability should be mentioned. Both see self-evaluation as an aspect of professionalism, and the line between the two approaches is not a sharp one. The first focuses on interactions between teachers, and makes use to a greater or lesser extent of interpretive, contextual approaches to evaluation and case study. This is very much a matter for the individual school rather than the school system, and heavy demands will be made on staff time. The services of a specialist evaluator or consultant may be advisable. Detailed notes on school self assessment procedures have been prepared by Frith and Macintosh (1980). A thoughtful, responsive approach, funded by the Australian Curriculum Development Centre, is the Teachers as Evaluators Project (Hughes, Russell, McConachy, 1980). The aim is 'to provide teachers with the materials, skills and expertise to conduct their own evaluations', bearing in mind that 'it is crucial that early initiatives for an evaluation study come from the whole school staff'.

These are sensitive and responsible ways of instituting formal evaluation. But I have argued in the last chapter that they may have unexpected side effects, and cannot guarantee curriculum change. However enlightened and humanitarian the style of evaluation may be, there is no gainsaying the fact that evaluation occurs after the event, and cannot itself influence the practical performance of future events. However well a teacher may be able to evaluate himself and others, this is no assurance that he has acquired the idiom of the practical activity of solving curriculum problems. For practical knowledge cannot be 'evaluated', yet it is the only kind of knowledge which guarantees professional performance. Insofar as evaluation must inevitably apply only to technical knowledge of the activity, an attempt to change the curriculum as a result of an evaluation will be based on an abridged knowledge of curriculum activity.

A related approach focuses rather more deliberately on teachers in classrooms, and possibly on the individual teacher. This takes even more time, and may call for the elaborate apparatus of tape recorders, video recorders, teacher diaries, pupil comments and so on. There is a solemnity and self-consciousness about this rigmarole which would be risible were it not for the danger that so much self-contemplation might have harmful effects on a teacher's view of himself. In particular, these approaches seek to make explicit all those sub-routines and automatic responses which make up the intuitive, innate part of a practical activity: they make the concert pianist worry about his fingering. In the same category come efforts to reduce classroom process to concepts and rules, and so establish teaching technology as a new research field. Again, the fundamental error is to suppose that descriptions of activities adequately represent those activities. Lists of rules and procedures are detached from the personal context of the teacher. They are merely an abridgement of the activity proper, and learning them is again no assurance that the practical arts of teaching have been acquired. Furthermore, teaching is so complex that the perceptions offered by such approaches can only be rudimentary in the extreme:

> Even when methods are used that focus on, say teaching, the data provided is almost always a very slender slice of the reality that it is supposed to represent ... The richness and diversity of the classroom that the data represent is virtually impossible to imagine, hence the conclusions derived from such data are in a significant sense acontextual. (Eisner, 1979)

Despite the bold claims made for internal and self evaluation in schools, it is difficult to see how they can be substantiated. It is a great deal of work — and dangerous work at that — with no logical relevance to professional performance or to curriculum change. In any case, as House (1973) observes: 'What does a teacher have to gain from having his work examined? ... Do we have any serious evaluations of lawyers, or doctors, or cabdrivers? ... No one wants to be evaluated by anybody at any time'. But, it will be argued, evaluation there must be, since it is now a political imperative; and if there must be evaluation, these forms are preferable to performance testing.

I am not convinced, though, that there is a deep public desire for the kind of accountability advocated in the Green Paper, any more than there is for monetarist economic policies. My own experience of curriculum innovation in a school where entry was determined strictly by parental choice, and in competition with other comprehensives operating a traditional curriculum, is that parents seek a general reassurance that the school has a coherent, worked out view of its educational programme, and a particular readiness to interpret this for their child in the context of his or her school life. They rely not so much on detail and data, as on personal contact and an intuitive response to the school's continuing attempts to explain and advise. Confirmation of this comes from Elliott (1979b), who as director of another accountability project (the Social Science Research Council has committed considerable funds to accountability research) has interviewed parents about the way they assess schools: 'They are more concerned with the social relevance of their school's curriculum policies than with its productivity in the form of examination results'. Parents, Elliott found, did not see quantifiable information as central to evaluating the work of a school, and he found 'few parents wanting to see schools publishing their exam results'. As head of an 11-18 comprehensive school I made full exam results freely available, but I cannot recall a parent ever seeking to discuss them. Parents do not need an avalanche of data about schools: they sense that it is difficult to interpret out of context and an unsatisfactory basis for comparisons. They do, however, pay high regard to the attitudes of staff, both as individuals and as reflecting the school's rationale of the curriculum.

Not only are they intuitively right to do so: Bailey (1980) has argued that there are sound philosophical reasons for seeing teachers not as accountable to others, but to themselves. What parents look for is the extent to which teachers see themselves as educators: 'The tradition, associated more with morality than with legality, of *personal* accountability'. Bailey goes on to argue that such a teacher will seek the intellectual autonomy which we expect to see in a doctor:

> An autonomous teacher is ... not ungoverned. To claim to be autonomous is to claim to *be* governed in a special kind of way. An autonomous teacher does not ignore the wishes and interests of others — parents, pupils, governments and employers — but such a teacher does reserve the right to consider such wishes and interests in the light of appropriate criteria ... He might consider it proper to be subject in some matters to the judgment of his professional associates.

Bailey considers that the case for teacher autonomy rests on his possessing and pursuing a concept of general education since 'to be autonomous necessitates being acquainted with the ways of knowing and understanding which provide the most fundamental criteria of judging and comparing among imaginable and presented courses of action and belief'. Only through understanding such a concept of general education can teachers and schools 'liberate pupils from the present and the particular, not anchor them more tightly into these accidents of history, geography and social class'.

I find this a persuasive argument, which exposes the crude and misguided basis on which most present discussion of teacher accountability rests. It also makes explicit the educational values on which professionalism depends. And it shows that to define professionalism through self-evaluation is to miss the real point: professionalism is not just a matter of technical tricks, it is a matter of a defined educational stance. This concern with a view of education cannot be divorced from the work of a teacher, any more than a view of sickness and health can be divorced from that of a doctor. A doctor's professionalism does not rest in the assesments he makes after he has prescribed a treatment, but in the intentions which determine the kind of action he takes from the beginning: 'A doctor must act autonomously in judging what to do for a patient, otherwise he is not really acting as a doctor' (Bailey, 1980). So the teacher must ultimately depend on his understanding of education as something which will transform his pupils' view of the world, and on his practical knowledge of the activity of teaching. And these two are, as Oakeshott has argued, a continuous whole: our cultural inheritance 'cannot be taught overtly, by precept, because it comprises what is required to animate precept; but it may be taught in everything that is taught' (Oakeshott, 1967).

Accountability, then, does not lie in the external monitoring of schools, nor in the technical verbiage of self evaluation. It lies in teacher autonomy as an educational concept, and it is through exploring and deploying that concept that curriculum change will be brought about. I shall discuss the implications of this briefly in the last section of this chapter.

Before leaving the subject of accountability, there is a final question to ask. If parents and teachers do not want accountability based on evaluation, who does? Well, it has an attraction for administrators, who tend to feel that numbers represent a kind of security. But they need the support of politicians, and as it is realised that evaluation is both expensive and unreliable, political support for evaluative accountability may wane. As W. Taylor (1976) has written:

> In the last analysis, accountability is a chimera. If teachers are already accepting the goals of those to whom they are deemed to be accountable, and are reasonably competent in implementing those goals, then such supervision is largely unnecessary. If the goals are confused, or teachers do not accept them or are incompetent to pursue them, then supervision will not secure clarity, acceptance or competence.

What matters are the goals themselves, and hence the teacher's accountability to himself.

Support for school evaluation also comes from academics who see it as a fruitful form of research. This will be true not only of those committed to the development of 'measures' for assessing school performance, but also of those who see teaching and learning as activities which can be broken into components and reduced to mechanisms. It is convenient to look a little further at these issues in my final section.

Examinations

It could be argued that parents and employers have long sought examination results as a measure of accountability. Yet it is doubtful if these have been seen, until recently, as other than a measure of pupil performance. My experience is that parents are much readier to attribute examination disappointment to the child rather than the school, rightly or wrongly. And although employers' organisations are often eloquent on the need for examination standards, schools know that most employers attach at least as much importance to the interview and the personal view of school staff.

Even so, no discussion of evaluation would be complete without reference to the problems of external examination and in particular of examining at sixteen plus. The educational difficulty is easily stated. In education we are concerned with states of mind, but examinations — like all evaluations — are to do with evidence for states of mind. And the connection between the two has no logical reality, and may be extremely tenous in practice. So public examinations are, in the nature of things, bound to be imperfect, and in a perfect world we should be wise to dispose of them.

We must accept, though, that even if teachers could unilaterally abolish O-level and CSE, employers and others would quickly fill the breach and invent their own. And these are likely to be even more imperfect than the examinations we have. It is pointless, therefore, to lament the huge sums spent on public examinations: they are an aspect of our society, and of our reluctance to rely on our own judgments of pupils, and on pupils' judgments of themselves. And this reluctance is peculiarly common among teachers. Whatever our private view (and I hold no brief for any form of evaluation, except the professional judgments of teachers themselves), we must accept that society pays for its collective fears and prejudices.

What kind of examination, then, will be the least imperfect? The obvious answer is: that kind which, with the least effort and expense, most acceptably gratifies the public need for examinations without introducing too great a risk of misleading results. All examinations are misleading: it is widely agreed that 'terminal examinations both at school and university are poor predictors of future academic success'

(Black, 1980). But some styles of examining are less misleading, and the minimum necessary number of these would seem to be the solution to adopt.

Curiously, though, many who voice their dissatisfaction with the present system of examining would replace it by systems which would lead to much more pupil evaluation, not less. It is argued that since comprehensive schools should offer pupils a broad range of educational experiences, this should be matched by a broad system of evaluation. Thus a CEO writes:

> The increased public interest in school examination results should be seized upon, and should lead to the introduction of proper criteria references as measures of performance and attainment for all pupils in their final year. The criteria used should be fit to show beyond argument that the decade or more the pupils have spent at school has been to good purpose and given them a good preparation for employment and the use of their future leisure time. (Henley, 1979)

Alas, evaluation is not as easy as this, because education is not as tidy as this. There are no 'proper criteria references' which demonstrate learning 'beyond argument'. The dream has been pursued by NAEP in North America, by the APU in the UK, and will doubtless continue to be pursued by the NFER and other agencies all the while someone is prepared to provide the finance for such undertakings.

One can, however, see that the idea of summarising a pupil's education in some final evaluative instrument would appeal to the administrative mind. What is surprising is to find exactly the same argument advanced on educational grounds:

> It is our argument, and that of the contributors to this book, that ... there must be a serious recording of the outcome of education at the end of the compulsory stage. For each individual this outcome is represented by the competencies, attributes, interests and purposes with which he or she faces the problems and opportunities of adult life. (Burgess and Adams, 1980)

What these writers seek 'are not so much terminal measures of achievement to be used for selection purposes as kinds of assessment which provide teachers, parents and pupils with guidance'. But the issue is not the use to which assessments are put, but the act of assessing: and if one is to assess the whole range of 'competencies, attributes, interests and purposes' then it would seem more confidence is being placed in assessment systems than could possibly be justified. In the event, what is being advocated is 'a statement which every sixteen year old will have on leaving school, showing his experience, competence, interests and purposes'. Two years earlier, each pupil will plan a 'programme of work', based on his understanding of himself. It is acknowledged that this is 'a difficulty to most people'. In fact, the evidence of option schemes is that pupils have only the scantiest knowledge of themselves and their aspirations at fourteen, but this does not deter these writers from describing their proposal as 'a new approach to the curriculum'. The planning of pupils' programmes would be reviewed by 'an external validating board' which would include such worthies as the chairmen of the chamber of commerce and trades council. The programmes would 'greatly increase the "relevance" ... missing from school at present'. The contention is that 'What we need to know about education is the difference which a particular course or programme has made to those who have followed it'.

The idea of contracted student programmes is borrowed from some English experiments in higher education. In the USA, 'contracts with students' have been explored with poorly motivated or disadvantaged junior high school students, but there are difficulties (Quinto and McKenna, 1977). Any preordinate statement of objectives is reductionist, and the objectives tend to be seen as more important than the process. Contracts tend to take 'more time and effort than do most conventional programmes'. But the fundamental objection to this proposal is two-fold. First, the emphasis on 'relevance' indicates a misconception of what education is about; and second, there is a misplaced faith in the ability of assessment devices to describe the process of education, and in the 'outcomes of education' to describe what school is for. As John Holt (1970) has noticed, education is more important than its determinable outcomes:

> There is no reason except to relieve our own anxieties and insecurity that we should constantly know what children are learning. What true education requires of us is faith and courage — faith that children want to make sense out of life and will work hard at it, courage to let them do it without continually poking, prodding and meddling.

The fact that schools should be encouraged to develop a range of personal and social responses in pupils, and a broader view of the curriculum than that of the 1902 grammar school, is not a good argument for trying to assess all these things. As Stake pointed out, at the height of the American accountability movement, 'one of the most serious mistakes would be to assume because there is a real and large need for information — that information will be worth the money it will cost. Or even that it is possible to get information truly relevant to the need' (Stake, 1976). There is no point in making assessments which are not widely acceptable, or which, for the sake of comprehensiveness, reduce a range of talents to a few numbers on a card. Devices like a Record of Personal Experience (Stansbury, 1980) were found, in a Schools Council study, to have limited acceptability, and a school offering a 'profile' as a sixteen plus output found that 'local employers ... place greater emphasis upon an interview than they do upon any written material. The few who are prepared to persevere with profiles are those who have had direct contacts with parents' (Fletcher, 1980). The Scottish SCRE profile system (SCRE, 1977) is typical of this approach, but amounts to little more than a few grade numbers on a card. The Stansbury proposal avoids this reductionism by using 'primary unprocessed material' (Stansbury, 1980), and might well act as a motivating device in a school where non-academic pupils had to overcome the labelling mechanisms of ability bands and option systems. But Stansbury is certainly right to see it only as a complement to a system of examinations and reports. The real answer is not in examination and assessment systems, but in a common curriculum which offers worthwhile opportunities for learning to all pupils. To suppose that the adoption of such systems will itself promote such a curriculum is to put the cart before the horse. Change comes not from better or different systems of evaluation, but from better thinking and curriculum planning.

The solution to the examinations problem should, I think, be sought not on maximalist but on minimalist lines. But if the assessment is of too restrictive a nature, as in narrow APU testing of only English, mathematics and science, there is the risk that the pressure on schools for a narrower curriculum will be hard to resist. There is, in fact, no reason why the existing O-level/CSE system at sixteen plus cannot be used for the public assessment of a common curriculum. In a mixed 11-18 comprehensive operating a common 11-16 curriculum, and in a parental choice area, the 1979 fifth-year group secured an average of over seven subject grades per pupil; ninety-four per cent obtained five or more grades in a range of subjects, while thirty per cent obtained five or more O-level grades ABC or CSE grade 1s (Seddon, 1979).

The Schools Council's proposal for a common system of examining at sixteen plus might, or might not, prove more amenable than what we have already. It depends on how it is done, and the thinking of the Secretary of State on the subject is obscure. Certainly the notion that O-level represents some absolute unwavering standard, like the metric units of the National Physical Laboratory, is nonsense.

But it is also true that examination boards, while recognising the essentially subjective nature of their art, take great pains to sustain comparability between boards and over time (see, for example, Bardell, Forrest and Shoesmith, 1978). This judgmental approach to assessment, which makes explicit the value decisions on which all assessment rests, is infinitely preferable to the bogus objectivity of performance testing. It is also important to note the thoughtful and sensitive forms of examination which O-level and CSE boards have developed in recent years. A good example is the interboard CSE examination in history developed for the Schools Council History 13-16 Project (itself an admirable school-linked curriculum development project) by the Southern Regional Examinations Board (Macintosh, 1979). The questions confront candidates with original sources as pieces of historical evidence, and answers are assessed for such qualities as interpretation, background, continuity, causal explanation and judgment. The corresponding O-level examination works on similar lines.

These are Mode 1 examinations, externally set and marked. Examinations in Modes 2 and 3 allow greater school involvement and hence more flexibility. The potential of these forms of public examination has yet to be properly exploited in the UK. An interesting example of a more school-based public system of examination is that in Queensland, Australia — not least because Queensland is politically a notably conservative State. In July 1969 Queensland appointed the Radford Committee to review the existing public examination system, which was broadly similar to that of GCE O and A-level. By December 1970 it had reported, and its recommendations had been accepted. (The Schools Council's interminable negotiations on a common sixteen plus examining system seem tortuous in comparison.) A Board of Secondary School Studies was constituted, to moderate internally assessed examinations set and conducted by schools. The new scheme was studied a few years later (Campbell *et al.* 1975). Some criticisms were made, but the Campbell study noted that 'The present scheme of moderated teacher assessments has stimulated the professional growth of school administrators and teachers, and has fostered a school identity'. In 1978 a Parliamentary Select Committee recommended that 'a return to external examinations should not be considered ... The principle of school based assessment should be supported' (Berkeley, 1980). The result of these reforms has not been, as some in the UK might suppose, the total collapse of standards and of civilisation as Queenslanders know it. On the contrary, although there is 'an absence of examination mania', there is 'a much greater chance for schools to prepare their own teaching programmes' (Berkeley, 1980).

These Australian reforms show what can be done to improve the existing styles of examination, and there are many schools in the UK with valuable experience of Mode 3 work. There are also enterprising examination administrators and curriculum developers who can point to the success of similar programmes on a small scale. What there are not is an understanding of how acceptable styles of examination can be made to serve the curriculum, and politicians with the leadership and imagination to initiate such reforms. It should be noted that the Australians, through the work of their Curriculum Development Centre (Skilbeck, 1980) are also actively pursuing the development of a common curriculum on a national basis, locally interpreted. There is much to be said for a closer look at Australian work on curriculum and examinations: in many ways it has much more to offer us, and is more in keeping with our own development of national education, than the production-model orientation of many North American imports like performance testing.

Evaluation, Research and Curriculum Change

Evaluation presents a rich field to the educational researcher. Nisbet (1974) argued that curriculum evaluation is an extension of educational research, making use of the same methods and skills. MacDonald (1976) accepts this, while pointing out that 'The researcher is free to select his questions, and to seek answers to them'. But the evaluator must not 'limit his inquiries to those which satisfy the critical canons of conventional research'. Three widely publicised pieces of research are all in effect evaluation studies, using the conventional science-inspired methods about which MacDonald was voicing reservations. On the face of it, this style of research appears to offer access to ineluctable truths. But closer study reveals the assumptions and simplicities on which such research must rest. An example to mention first would be Bennett's study of primary school teaching: a study based on a small sample, and categorising teaching styles into a few types to fit the research techniques (Bennett, 1976). Chanan's comment (1976) on this study makes a sound point:

> It is a complete illusion to suppose that research gains its credibility from proving anything, even if it does really happen to prove things. Almost no one who makes use of it looks closely at the evidence ...

Social research must be understood as primarily an ideological rather than scientific phenomenon.

Extreme care is needed in drawing any conclusions from classroom interaction research: the concepts, the sampling, the statistical treatment are all problematic, and to evaluate such a complex activity as teaching by research of this kind is to misunderstand the nature of reality.

A second example is the Rutter research (Rutter *et al.*, 1979), which uses the same model of 'a production function (i.e. pupil measured achievement) resulting from input factors' (Shaw, 1980). The statistical basis of this research has been challenged by a number of writers (Goldstein 1980, Preece 1980) and need not concern us here. The point is that, as with all research in this pseudo-scientific tradition, it leaves out most of the issues which really matter. Golby (1980) gets to the heart of the matter:

> Firstly, the curriculum of the secondary school has not been address-ed. This is unfortunate since the curriculum is the single most impor-tant set of variables in the educational process ... Secondly, Rutter's at-tempt to isolate discernible features of school organisation, and their relationships to outcomes, provides percepts without the necessary ac-companying analysis of educational concepts ... Thirdly, I believe ge-nuine educational research must call upon a general theory of learning and teaching ...

Despite the crudity of its output measures and the dubious research method on which it depends, the Rutter study is already being seen as an evaluation of secondary schools and its conclusions used to sup-port changes.

A particularly searching criticism of this style of curriculum evaluation has been made by Reid (1979), who examines Newbold's research on ability grouping at Banbury School (Newbold, 1977). This third example exhibits the same reductionist approach: 'It is not based on a conception of how a social or educational system works ... (There is) a search for "key variables" ... There is a lack of concern with ... such notions as "meaning" or "purpose" ' (Reid, 1979). Anomalies which fail to fit the research are dropped from the analysis: but 'The researcher's "anomalies" are the teacher's realities'. This kind of research does little to help teachers solve cur-riculum problems:

> Improvements in the quality of teacher education and of teaching in our schools are not dependent upon the outcomes of large quantities of newly-commissioned research, or waiting upon some conceptual or

methodological breakthrough in understanding or technique. Teacher education and teaching could both be improved on the basis of knowledge currently available, given the political will to devote resources to this ... We already know far more than we can use. (W. Taylor, 1978)

I have noted that an important fillip to the DES advocacy of national monitoring was given by the unequivocal support accorded to it by the Bullock Report (1975) on the teaching of English. The Bullock emphasis on 'realistic sampling of the skills' now seems hard to reconcile with its enthusiasm for an expressive approach to language and a view of language as a curriculum influence which has generally pleased language specialists. It is worth remarking, though, that the theory of 'language across the curriculum' favoured by Bullock stems, as Williams (1977) has shown, from an approach to language worked out by Britton and others in the 1960s (see, for example, Britton, 1967). This approach was a reaction against the 'production model' favoured by the Americans, yet ended up with a mechanistic element:

> This dislike of ... 'impersonal' language uses in education is evident in the writings of the Writing Research Unit from the beginning, placing them firmly in the English-teaching ethos of the 1960s, which reacted against the 'new technology' and the predominance of science in the post-Sputnik era, and staked everything on an intra-rather than an inter-personal approach. But technology and its 'systems' crept in even here ... It was the *ethno-* and *psycho*-linguistics ... which attracted ... A *model* of language functions was deemed necessary, to replace the verbal description of earlier formulations. The Project had become 'scientific'. (Williams, 1977).

The theory which ultimately found its way into the Bullock Report was a psychological theory of language (and unsupported, as Williams shows, by any experimental data). It was therefore an easy step for Bullock to support the kind of testing so widely advocated and developed by psychologists. For although the doctrine of 'language across the curriculum' is presented as nothing less than a theory of curriculum, it is in fact based on empirical inquiry rather than a conceptual inquiry into educational issues. The underlying linguistic model attempts to slice the complexities of language into the categories and the components of science-inspired research, and this mechanistic approach shows through in the Bullock proposals for teacher training as well as in the emphasis on testing. Holbrook (1980) has described the Bullock Report as 'a serious offence to education, learning and research', and remarks that the linguistic theory it advocates will be as useful in training teachers as studying the principles of mechanics is to a child learning to ride a bicycle. The analogy is a shrewd one, for teaching and cycling both depend on practical knowledge, and the sterile theory masquerading as technical knowledge can never inform the activity itself. Yet it is precisely this kind of theory which will — and does — result from evaluation studies. As Holbrook points out, what happens in primary schools is 'far more complex and rich than learning to use verbal skills in communication'. The Bullock Report is

> dominated by theory, and bad theory at that — of intrusions into arts subjects from linguistics, disciplines based on a physicalist psychology, even with neuro-physiology and behaviourism in the background — at a time when the essential failure of such disciplines to explain consciousness and experience was being widely recognised and discussed.

Yet Bullock is still widely regarded — particularly by HMI — as the authoritative statement on a key area of the curriculum. It is important not only to challenge its assumptions that a particular view of language is appropriate to all disciplines — as Williams (1977) notes, the team which inspired the Bullock doctrine wanted 'to graft uses of language ... from their own subject area to all the others in the curriculum, without any research into the concepts of other disciplines to find out what *kind* of language best advances the pupil's knowledge of them' — it is also important to record the congruence between the mechanistic approach of Bullock and the performance testing movement. The link between Bullock and the APU, described in chapter three, shows the pervasive influence of utilitarian approaches to education by means of evaluation.

Two quite different studies of curriculum renewal in schools bear out the view that an undue emphasis on evaluation may be unhelpful. Green (1980) reports how the Independent Learning in Science Project (ILIS) began as an initiative among a group of schools. On applying to the Schools Council for a five-year support programme, 'much play was made ... of the need for objective evaluation, whatever that might mean or achieve'. The council rejected the ILIS request. Green comments:

> The continuing emergence of schemes of independent learning in science is, no doubt, in part based on a considered evaluation of the work that has been documented over the years, but the final decision (in schools) ... is much more likely to be traceable to what can perhaps be called 'gut evaluation' — an inner perception that it makes sense;

consistency with fundamental educational aims; a stirring of the imagination; that conglomeration of sentiments and values, never quite sorted out, but which nevertheless informs and determines many of life's major decisions.

No one who has ever engaged in thorough-going curriculum innovation can doubt that Green's intuitions are right, and have very little to do with the curious notion of 'objective evaluation'.

A second example of the danger of schools relying on easily-assembled data as the basis of evaluation comes from Weston's study (1979) of curriculum change in a 13-18 comprehensive school. The Schools Council Integrated Science Project (SCISP) had been adopted in the fourth and fifth year curriculum in 1972. A new headmaster arrived in 1974, and 'expressed considerable interest in the programme ... but directed the attention of the department to the need for evaluation'. The 'evaluation' took the form of a superficial look at the examination results. By March 1976, without any adequate consideration of the issues, SCISP was dead: 'A decision was formally adopted ... that the third year of 1977/78 would study separate sciences'. The rhetoric of 'evaluation' led directly to the abandonment of a curriculum innovation of arguably considerable educational merit. Instead of looking at the way the science staff were tackling the curriculum problems generated by SCISP, the head and staff virtually drifted into a decision (as Weston makes clear) which placed little value on all the innovatory work already completed.

Weston's study is itself an evaluation. It enables us to look at a school's decisions and ask: Were they good decisions? But it is refreshing to note that it is not described as an evaluation, possibly because it eschews quantitative methods and the search for measures of performance, and instead offers a straightforward account of what was observed, and lets us see what kind of judgments the observer brought to her observations. It could be termed a 'case study', but there has been so much rhetoric and posturing about this form of inquiry that it is easy to forget it can be carried out in a perfectly naturalistic way.

I have argued that evaluation, in that it looks only at the technical and not the practical knowledge associated with an action, can lead to a misleading view of theory in relation to action. It seems to me that exactly the same error can arise with the kind of self-evaluation identified by Stenhouse with his concept of the 'teacher as researcher' (1975):

> Effective curriculum development of the highest quality depends
> upon the capacity of teachers to take a research stance to their own

teaching. By a research stance I mean a disposition to examine one's own practice critically and systematically.

Stenhouse has explained that this concept arose from difficulties encountered in introducing the methods of the Humanities Curriculum project in schools: 'teacher development grew from the teachers' monitoring their own performance against specific criteria set out in the project handbook. From this self-monitoring grew the concept of teacher as researcher' (Stenhouse, 1981).

It is the specificity and formality of the 'teacher as researcher' concept which I find uncongenial. My experience is that the degree of precision and systematisation associated with the activity of research is not appropriate to the activity of teaching and — to generalise — to the defining and solving of curriculum problems. Certainly the teacher must have a critical view of what he does: as Reid (1978) has put it, 'The basic need is common to all problem solving, practical and theoretic: to establish and maintain a critical tradition within which the worthwhileness of proposals and solutions can be scrutinised'. Such a tradition must be an innate part of a practical activity like teaching: 'Only the theoretic can offer to the practitioner explanations and prescriptions rather than statements and conclusions empty of consequences' (Reid, 1979). But there is an intuitive, idiomatic aspect to curriculum activity which transcends the mechanism of self-reflection, and the systematic tidiness associated with public research: 'Coming to know what one wants is partly a decision and partly a discovery' (Hampshire, 1959). There is also something disturbingly solipsistic about the 'teacher as researcher' model, and it is no surprise that it has led to a focusing on the individual teacher in his classroom rather than the study of teachers working together to develop new insights and strategies.

The key emphasis must, I think, be placed on a more naturalistic interpretation of systematic theory, and one which focuses on the intentions which teachers bring to their actions: on what happens before the event, rather than too much scrutiny of its effects: 'Theory as systematic inquiry sets out to establish what is, in fact, the case and to provide perspectives for understanding how and why things work the way they do' (Reid, 1978). What underlies curriculum change is not an inclination towards research, but something rather broader — a view of theory as an intrinsic element of practice, deriving from it and informing it but never separate from it:

A tradition of practical reasoning is built up through extending, elaborating and refining the criteria by which actions are to be justified, and showing how these criteria are to be weighed in practical

situations. The growth of the tradition is made possible by the colla-
tion and discussion of examples of practice, by the insights of gifted individuals and the discovery of new possibilities through experimenta-
tion. The result is a formal and accessible body of knowledge, not of a
commonsense nature, about how to engage in effective deliberation.
(Reid, 1978).

What makes formal evaluation such a damaging activity — as opposed to informal evaluation as a unified aspect of practice — is that it in-
hibits practical reasoning by seeking the technical apparatus of rules
and procedures. The need is for deliberation, not evaluation.

A final example might perhaps make the point clear. Writing of the
need for pupil evaluation and for teachers to enter the results on
pupil record cards, Harlen (1978) notes that teachers are, even so,
reluctant to use other teachers' records, often arguing 'they do not
want to be biased by what others say'. Harlen is puzzled by this
'mistrust of other teachers' observations about children', and feels
'every piece of information is useful in building up the picture'. But
this is to miss the point: what teachers know is that the kind of information that can be written on cards about children is, like any evaluation, simply an abridgment of a complex world of sensations, actions and imaginings. And most records are not so much an abridgment as a travesty of these things. Teachers know that what matters
about a child is what *cannot* be evaluated and written down; all the
practical knowledge which is instantiated by the act of teaching. This
is not an argument for the abolition of records, but it does suggest
that they should be regarded as piecemeal, diminished accounts of a
whole spectrum of responses and qualities, and should therefore be
treated with a proper reserve. To do otherwise is to misunderstand
the excitement and optimism which should characterise teaching and
learning.

Evaluation, Assessment and the Teacher

This book must end where learning begins: with the encounter between teacher and learner, and the efforts of the teacher to improve
his practice and that of his school. It is easy to forget when so much
effort is being devoted to the technology of formal assessment, that
without an informed, unceasing appraisal of the effects of his actions,
no teacher can ever act as an effective professional agent. All teachers
evaluate informally, and the more aware they are of the exchanges
between themselves and their pupils the better teachers they will

become. But the emphasis on formal evaluation — like the fashion in the seventies to stress pastoral care as a separate activity — has the effect of limiting the professional view teachers must have of themselves. All teachers are in the pastoral care business, and — in the sense that no practical activity can be successfully performed without making thinking a part of doing — all teachers are in the evaluating business.

But it is essential not to confuse this kind of self-knowledge with a superficial self-consciousness. There are no short cuts to self-knowledge: it is all of a piece with becoming an autonomous person, and this — as Bailey (1980) has argued — rests on the development of mind; on ways of knowing, doing and understanding. The enthusiasm for promoting self evaluation and self assessment by conscious recall of acts and events is a quite different activity, which cannot throw light on the fundamental idiom which is the professional mark of the teacher. There are some similarities here with the American fashion to acquire self-knowledge by popularising the theories and therapies of psychologists. Rosen (1979), in his interesting study of what he terms 'psychobabble', suggests that the casual use of this language 'transforms self-understanding, which each must gain gradually through experience and analysis, into tokens of self-understanding that can be exchanged between people, but without any clear psychological value'. He sees this as part of 'the current narcissism engendered by the idea of just "being oneself"', and ultimately an obstruction to effective self understanding.

Clarity about the limitations of self evaluation is so important that I shall draw a further example from an activity quite different from teaching, yet related to it partly because it involves the idea of a performance, and partly because it is an activity only to be understood in terms of the practical knowledge which makes it possible. An article discussing the work of the conductor Simon Rattle, (*Guardian*, 20 December, 1980) remarks on his 'mysterious ability' for producing good performances from orchestras, and 'to see himself from the outside, which is a requisite for any good performer. He knows how good he is, but he is absolutely not conceited'. Rattle is quoted as saying 'The basic rudiments of conducting you could teach to a chimp in five minutes' — this is part of the technical knowledge of the action, along with a mastery of the score and a well developed ear. And he is surely right to see this as only a minor aspect of the business. What is difficult is 'the amount of give and take' — practical knowledge of what it is to conduct an orchestra of many different individuals, which is not wholly unlike the work of a teacher in his classroom. A key element is an atmosphere 'where nobody is trying to prove anything to anybody else. It's totally relaxed. I don't feel I have to impress. They don't feel they have to endlessly question. One can get on with the job. Each side is learning each other's limitations as well as strengths ... It's to do with that flexibility'. In particular, Rattle finds 'One must feel as though it's the most natural thing in the world — like breathing. The minute you get self-conscious, it's impossible'.

Self-consciousness stems from a dependence on the evaluations of others: self knowledge — knowing 'how good' you are — comes from an understanding of how to judge yourself in your own terms. Although it leads to performing one's professional activity as if it were a 'natural thing', it is not the result of doing what comes naturally. It is not mere intuitionism. It is the result of getting on the inside of the activity, by doing it thoughtfully — by acquiring 'the most fundamental criteria of judging and comparing among imaginable and presentable courses of action and belief' (Bailey, 1980). Thus the autonomous teacher does not need to be labelled 'the teacher as researcher' or 'the teacher as evaluator' — he is the teacher as teacher — as one who has a broad enough understanding to have acquired the idiom of the activity of teaching.

In arguing, therefore, that an emphasis on formal evaluation is an unhelpful approach to teacher and curriculum improvement, I am not suggesting teachers may sink into apathy and do the first thing which comes into their head. Quite the reverse: the autonomous teacher is a dedicated professional who realises that the more you know, the more you realise how little you know. He sees his own subject specialism not as a confining cage for his thoughts, but as a springboard from which he can explore other forms of cultural action. He seeks self understanding by developing his personal understanding; he learns about his own strengths and weaknesses by planning, deliberating and acting along with other professionals.

What, then, should be the place of formal assessment in schools? I do not see great value in the construction of elaborate assessment systems within schools. Much of a teacher's assessment will arise from what he sees of his pupils' work. But he will also invent tests to match the work in hand, and perhaps occassionally make use of prepared test material. Given the reality of external examinations at sixteen plus, he will, in due course, introduce his pupils to the techniques which lead to examination success. The hope, however, must be that sixteen plus examinations can be Mode 3, school-based exercises with a substantial element of course work.

In a thoughtful article on the evils of our present examination system, a chief education officer laments our dependence on it and suggests that the alternative is 'to encourage and disseminate as widely as possible the enhancement of the teacher's assessment techniques' (Cruise, 1980). But I am not convinced that this is the answer, or, indeed, that the answer lies in the acquisition of any kind of technique in itself. The more one studies assessment, the more evident it is that the subjectivity of the assessor is inescapable. Improvement and confidence can come only from an enhanced professionalism, which must in turn be built on a deeper understanding of the nature of curriculum problems.

Is there, then, no place for the apparatus of evaluation? I think the American experience of psychometric styles of evaluation, and — for that matter — the gulf between the aspirations of the APU in this country and its actual outcomes, must be sufficient to raise the gravest doubts about the value of monitoring performance by means of standardised tests. It is worth noting that a survey by a visiting American academic (Gooding, 1980) of teachers in north west England shows that

> sixty-five cent are generally opposed to national achievement testing in the schools ... fifty per cent of the teachers believed that a system of national achievement testing could lead to a more test-orientated curriculum ... The majority of those surveyed were of the opinion that they had not been adequately informed or consulted with respect to the design of the (APU's) testing programme.

Is school self-study, then, the answer if curriculum improvement is sought? The difficulty is that all evaluative instruments are inherently reductionist, since they can examine only the technical aspects of school activity. There are also the dangers, in Oakeshott's telling phrase, which can result from giving habit the role of critic. Neither does it follow that evaluation, which is the servant of past actions, can help us to become the master of new and better ones. Even so, it may be that a school self-study exercise could, if appropriately handled, lead on to a deeper questioning and to new styles of professional action The danger about approaches which, for example, urge head teachers to 'follow a class round the school for a day' (Oxfordshire Education Department, 1979) is that they do not in themselves lead to a study of fundamental issues. No amount of observation can tell us what pupils have *actually* learnt: no evaluation can be separated from some subjective opinion. And curriculum planning should start not with a catalogue of perceived inadequacies but with some consideration of the nature of education itself.

It is disturbing, too, to note the readiness with which schools, administrators and academics have moved into what have already been dubbed 'the evaluating eighties'. Some schools have appointed a senior member of staff to act as the 'evaluator', collecting data and fostering self evaluation. There is also a move to urge the adoption of models of 'good practice', and to instal techniques of 'sound management'. Evaluation is seen as a way in which deficiencies can be identified and eliminated, much as a faulty machine can be replaced on a production line. But schools are interactive organisms; teachers are involved in an idiomatic activity; and curriculum is a form of life. Worthwhile change can result only from the inside, and from a careful study of fundamental issues. One must agree with Stenhouse (1981) that 'The view of curriculum development, to which I am not sympathetic, seems to be that schooling can be improved if teachers adopt or develop curriculum innovations which embody better practice.'

I would argue, then, that the effort currently devoted to self evaluation exercises might be better spent on other forms of school-based curriculum development. The research need is not to refine still further the instruments of testing and assessing, but to study the way in which teachers come together to think about curriculum issues, and the way in which a curriculum problem can be described and handled. Such a process will, in the nature of things, extend our understanding of what goes on in schools: if you like, it will lead to new forms of evaluation. But the time may have come to subject the word 'evaluation' to a self-denying ordinance, and rely instead on a whole range of terms which bring out the subjective nature of the activity, without the association of scientific certainty: judgment, inquiry, appraisal, study, account are all suitable. Eisner (1980) has suggested the term *educational criticism*.

> We need to use an approach to educational evaluation that capitalises on our human capacity to come to know reality in its multi-dimensional richness. The reduction of this richness to a single symbol system is an impoverishment of our ability to understand its multiple features.

We come to these forms of evaluation not by the pursuit of evaluation for its own sake, but by pursuing the activity of education. Singling out evaluation as a separate activity is to distort matters, just as a religious heresy was once seen as a distortion of the truth by elaborating a part at the expense of the whole. We may challenge the case for such an elaboration of educational evaluation on at least three grounds. First, all evaluation is ultimately based on opinion; by disguising this truth with the rituals of science, whether psychological or anthropological, we deceive and confuse ourselves, and allow our attention to be diverted from the real point — the intention which underlies our activity, and the justification for it. Second, evaluation is only weakly connected to the action it purports to assess, and can therefore lead to the generation of misleading theory and the mistaken view that evaluation can, of itself, promote change. If it does do so, it is the result of our imaginative intervention, and our consideration of underlying intentions. And third, the notion that evaluation rests upon some 'right to know' is but assertion 'of a particular political or moral position', for, like any 'right', it is 'contestable .. in the substantive claims made under its banner' (Pring, 1979). There is much talk of the need for evaluation: but the political or moral basis on which such a need depends is by no means always clear.

I would argue, therefore, that to give evaluation a disproportionate prominence may divert our reforming energies from more profitable approaches. Gratzer (1979), in discussing the rather inflated view many academics attach to research, mentions a cartoon he saw at an American university. Two Roman soldiers are watching the crucifixion. One says, 'They say he was a great teacher'. 'Yes,', says the other, 'but he didn't publish anything'. The caption could easily have read, 'They say he was a great innovator'. 'Yes, but he didn't evaluate anything'. Too much emphasis on evaluation — or on research, for that matter — will detract from the importance of doing: of the action itself.

Evaluation is an activity which cannot be meaningfully separated from curriculum action, and which is best left to those committing the action and therefore privileged to judge it. Formal evaluation is a needlessly elaborated search for inaccessible truths, and one which substitutes the drab routines of assessment and categorisation for the creative pleasures of planning, teaching and learning. If instead we can promote the concept of the teacher as an autonomous professional, accountable to himself as a reasoning person, then curriculum renewal will become a part of professionalism and the act of teaching will be a natural expression of the teacher's self understanding. And this is likely to be more enlightening and more pleasurable than an attempt to unravel the logic of past events. Maynard Keynes should have the last word: 'We have been trained too long to strive and not to enjoy'.

BIBLIOGRAPHY

ASSESSMENT OF PERFORMANCE UNIT (Department of Education and Science):
(1978) *Monitoring Mathematics*
(1978) *Language Performance*
(1979) *Science Progress Report 1977-78*
(1979) *Appendix: List of Science Concepts and Knowledge*
(1980) *Exploratory Group on Personal and Social Development: Consultative Document*
(1980) *Primary Survey Report No 1*
(1980) *Foreign Language.*
ATKIN, J.M. (1980) *Government in the Classroom*, University of London Institute of Education.
AULD, R. (1976) *William Tyndale Junior and Infants' Schools Public Inquiry*, ILEA.

BABINGTON SMITH, C. (1961) *Evidence in Camera*, Penguin.
BAILEY, C. (1980) 'The autonomous teacher', in H. SOCKETT (ed.) *Accountability in the English Educational System*, Hodder and Stoughton.
BARDELL, G., FORREST, G. and SHOESMITH, D. (1978) *Comparability in GCE*, Joint Matriculation Board, Manchester.
BECHER, A. (1978) 'The shackles fall', *The Times Educational Supplement*, 10 February.
BECHER, A., ERAUT, M., BARTON, J., CANNING, A. and KNIGHT, J. (1980) *Accountability in the Middle Years of Schooling*, University of Sussex.
BECHER, A. and MACLURE, S. (1978) *Accountability in Education*, N.F.E.R.
BENNETT, N. (1976) *Teaching Styles and Pupil Progress*, Open Books.
BENNETT, N. and MCNAMARA, D. (1980) *Focus on Teaching*, Longman.
BERKELEY, G. (1980) 'An alternative approach to the assessment and certification of secondary students: the Queensland experience', mimeo, University of London Institute of Education.
BLACK, H. (1980), 'The forms and functions of assessment', in T. BURGESS and E. ADAMS (eds) *Outcomes of Education*, Macmillan.
BLACK, P. and MARJORAM, T. (1979) *National and State Assessment in the U.S.A.*, Department of Education and Science.
BLOOM, B. (1956) (ed.) *The Taxonomy of Educational Objectives*, Longman.
BOULTER, P. (1978), 'Week by week', *Education*, 28 April.
BRIGHOUSE, T. (1979) 'The four yearly school report', mimeo, Oxfordshire Education Committee.
BRITTON, J. (ed.) (1967) *Talking and Writing in Education*, University of London Institute of Education.
BROADFOOT, P. (1979) *Assessment, Schools and Society*, Methuen.
BROWN, R. (1980) 'A visit to the APU', *Journal of Curriculum Studies, 12*, 1.
BULLOCK REPORT, THE (1975) *A Language for Life*, H.M.S.O.
BURGESS, T. and ADAMS, E. (1980) *Outcomes of Education*, Macmillan.
BURSTALL, C. (1974) *Primary French in the Balance*, N.F.E.R.
BURSTALL, C. and KAY, B. (1978) *Assessment: the American Experience*, D.E.S.

CAMPBELL, W., BASSETT, G., CAMPBELL, M., COTTERELL, J., EVANS, G. and GRASSIE, M. (1975) *Some Consequences of the Radford Scheme for Schools, Teachers and Students in Queensland*, Australian Advisory Committee on Research and Development in Education.

CARTER, D. (1980) 'APU tests a mistake', *The Times Educational Supplement*, 27 June.

CHANAN, G. (1976) 'Adding up the statistics', letter in *The Times Educational Supplement*, 14 May.

CLARK, C. (1979) 'Education and behaviour modification', *Journal of Philosophy of Education*, Vol 13.

CLAXTON, G. (1980) 'The inner game of teaching', *The Times Educational Supplement*, 15 February.

COOPER, K. (1976) 'Curriculum evaluation: definition and boundaries', in D. Tawney (ed.) *Curriculum Evaluation Today*, Macmillan.

CORDING, J., BARNES, J., LEWINS, T., REAY, D. and GEE, G. (1980) 'Are we testing the right things?' *The Times Educational Supplement*, 27 June.

CRUISE, K. (1980) 'Week by week', *Education*, 21 November.

DAWSON, J. (1980) Communication to author.

DENNY, T. (1977) *Some Still Do: River Acres, Texas*, Case Studies in Science Education, Centre for Instructional Research and Curriculum Evaluation, University of Illinois.

DEPARTMENT OF EDUCATION AND SCIENCE: ·

(1974)   White Paper: *Educational Disadvantage and the Educational Needs of Immigrants*

(1977)   *Curriculum 11–16*, HMI/DES

(1977)   *Educating Our Children*, DES

(1977)   *Education in Schools: a Consultative Document* (The Green Paper), H.M.S.O.

(1978)   *Assessing the Performance of Pupils*, Report on Education, 93, August

(1978)   *Primary Education in England*, H.M.S.O.

(1979)   *Aspects of Secondary Education*, H.M.S.O.

(1980)   *A Framework for the School Curriculum*, H.M.S.O.

(1980)   *A View of the Curriculum* HMI/DES, H.M.S.O.

EGGLESTON, S.J. (1978) 'APU's yardstick for maths and morality', *Guardian*, 6 June.

EISNER, E. (1975) 'The perceptive eye: toward the reformation of educational evaluation', American Educational Research Association Meeting, Washington D.C.

EISNER, E. (1979) 'Humanistic trends and the curriculum field' in P.H. TAYLOR (ed.), *New Directions in Curriculum Studies*, Falmer Press.

EISNER, E. (1980) 'The impoverished mind' in *Curriculum*, autumn.

ELLIOTT, G. (1980) *Self Evaluation and the Teacher*, University of Hull with the Schools Council.

ELLIOTT, G. (1981) *School Self Evaluation — The Way Forward*, Mimeo, University of Hull.

ELLIOTT, J. (1978) 'Classroom accountability and the self-monitoring teacher' in W.Harlen (ed.), *Evaluation and the Teacher's Role*, Macmillan.

ELLIOTT, J. (1979a) 'Curriculum evaluation and the classroom' (mimeo), Cambridge Institute of Education.

ELLIOTT, J. (1979b) 'The case for school self-evaluation', *Forum*, autumn.

ELLIOTT, J. and ADELMAN, C. (1976) 'Innovation at the classroom level: a case study of the Ford Teaching Project', Unit 28, Course E 203, The Open University.

ELTON, L. (1980) 'Physics teaching in secondary schools', *Physics Education*, June.

ERLANDSON, D. (1973) 'Evaluation and an administrator's autonomy' in E. HOUSE (ed.), *School Evaluation: the Politics and the Process*, McCutchan.

FLETCHER, C. (1980) 'The Sutton Centre profile', in T.BURGESS and E. ADAMS (eds), *Outcomes of Education*, Macmillan.

FLORIDA PUBLIC SCHOOLS DISTRICTS (1976) *Legislative Concerns*, Florida, U.S.A.

FLYNN, J. (1972) 'Evaluation and the fate of innovations', *Educational Technology*, April.

FOSHAY, A. (1977) 'What's basic about the curriculum?' *Language Arts*, September.

FRITH, D. and MACINTOSH, H. (1980) *In-Service Training of Teachers in Assessment*, International Association for Educational Assessment.

GALTON, M. (1979) 'A constructive response to the APU', *Forum*, autumn.

GOLBY, M. (1980) 'On from Rutter: researching educational effectiveness', *Perspectives 1*, Exeter University School of Education.

GOLDSTEIN, H. (1979) 'The mystification of assessment', *Forum*, autumn.

GOLDSTEIN, H. (1980) *'Fifteen Thousand Hours: A Discussion'* University of London Institute of Education.

GOLDSTEIN, H. and BLINKHORN, S. (1977) 'Doubts about item banking', *Bull. of Brit. Psych. Soc.*, 30, 309–311.

GOODING, C.T. (1980) 'An American looks at teacher views of the APU', *Forum*, autumn.

GRATZER, W. (1979) 'Research: the enemy of scholarship', *Guardian*, 11 October.

GREEN, E. (1980) 'The Independent Learning in Science model of school-based curriculum development' in J EGGLESTON (ed.), *School-Based Curriculum Development in Britain*, Routledge and Kegan Paul.

GREENBAUM, W., GARET, M. and SOLOMON, E. (1977) *Measuring Educational Progress*, McGraw Hill.

HAMPSHIRE, S. (1959) *Thought and Action*, Chatto and Windus.

HARLEN, W. (1978) (Ed.) *Evaluation and the Teacher's Role*, Macmillan.

HARLEN, W. (1980) 'Accountability that is of benefit to schools', *Journal of Curriculum Studies*, spring.

HENDERSON, E. (1978) *The Evaluation of In-Service Training*, Croom Helm.

HENLEY, M. (1979) 'Week by week', *Education*, 19 October.

HIRST, P.H. (1965) 'Liberal education and the nature of knowledge', in R.ARCHAMBAULT (ed.) *Philosophical Analysis and Education*, Routledge and Kegan Paul.

HIRST, P.H. (1974) *Knowledge and the Curriculum*, Routledge and Kegan Paul.

HOFFMAN, B. (1962) *The Tyranny of Testing*, Collier Books, U.S.A.

HOLBROOK, D. (1980) *English for Meaning*, N.F.E.R.

HOLT, J. (1970) *The Underachieving School*, Pitman.

HOLT, M. (1978) *The Common Curriculum*, Routledge and Kegan Paul.

HOLT, M. (1979) *Regenerating the Curriculum*, Routledge and Kegan Paul.

HOUSE, E. (1973) *School Evaluation: the Politics and the Process*, McCutchan.

HOUSE, E., RIVERS, L. and STUFFELBEAM, D. (1974) *An Assessment of the Michigan Accountability System*, National Education Association, Washington D.C.

HUGHES, P., RUSSELL, N. and MCCONACHY, D. (1980) *Teachers as Evaluators Project: Discussion Papers*, Curriculum Development Centre, Canberra.

KAIDALOV, D. and SUIMENKO, E. (1979) *The Psychology of One-Man Management and Collegiality*, Moscow.

KAY, B. (1975) 'Monitoring School Performance', *Trends in Education*, July.

KELLNER, P. and CROWTHER-HUNT, LORD (1980) *The Civil Servants: an Inquiry into Britain's Ruling Class*, Macdonald.

KEMMIS, S. (1979) 'Nomothetic and idiographic approaches to the evaluation of learning' in P.H.TAYLOR (ed.), *New Directions in Curriculum Studies*, Falmer Press.

LACEY, C. and LAWTON, D. (1981) *Accountability and Evaluation*, Methuen.

LANGFORD, G. (1972) *Human Action*, Macmillan.

LANGFORD, G. (1973) 'The concept of education' in G. LANGFORD and D. O'CONNOR (eds), *New Essays in the Philosophy of Education*, Routledge and Kegan Paul.

LAVISKY, S. (1975) 'Problems and potentials of applied performance testing', Invited address, Northwest Regional Educational Laboratory, Oregon.

LAWTON, D. (1980) *The Politics of the School Curriculum*, Routledge and Kegan Paul.

LEONARD, M. (1977) 'Made to measure?', *The Times Educational Supplement*, 2 December.

LYMAN, R. *et al.* (1980) *The Humanities in American Life*, University of California Press.

MACDONALD, B. (1976) 'Evaluation and the control of education', in D. TAWNEY (ed.), *Curriculum Evaluation Today*, Macmillan.'

MACDONALD, B. (1977) 'The objectives model revisited: introduction' in D.Hamilton *et al.* (eds) *Beyond the Numbers Game*, Macmillan.

MACDONALD-ROSS, M. (1975) 'Behavioural objectives: a critical review' in M.GOLBY *et al.* (eds) *Curriculum Design*, Croom Helm.

MACINTOSH, H.G. (1979) *Schools Council History 13–16 Project CSE Examination: the 1979 Written Examination*, Southern Regional Examinations Board.

MCINTYRE, D. and BROWN, S. (1978) 'The conceptualisation of attainment', *British Educational Research Journal*, 4, 2.

MARJORAM, T. (1979) 'The APU', report of a speech in *Education*, 12 January.

NATIONAL ACADEMY OF EDUCATION (1979) *Improving Educational Achievement*, Washington D.C.

NATIONAL EDUCATION ASSOCIATION (1978) *Memorandum to Participants in the 1978 Regional Conference,* NEA Washington D.C.

NATIONAL FOUNDATION FOR EDUCATIONAL RESEARCH (1975) *Tests of Attainment in Mathematics in Schools,* N.F.E.R.

NATIONAL FOUNDATION FOR EDUCATIONAL RESEARCH (1979) 'Local authorities' and schools' item banking project' (LEASIB), leaflet R. 180, N.F.E.R.

NEAVE, G. (1980) 'Developments in Europe' in T.BURGESS and E.ADAMS (eds), *Outcomes of Education, Macmillan.*

NEWBOLD, D. (1977) *Ability Grouping: the Banbury Enquiry,* N.F.E.R.

NISBET, J. (1974) 'Educational research — the state of the art', paper presented at inaugural meeting of the British Educational Research Association.

NUTTALL, D. (1976) Letter in *The Times Educational Supplement,* 16 July.

NUTTALL, D. (1979) 'A rash attempt to measure changing standards', *Education,* 21 September.

OAKESHOTT, M. (1962) *Rationalism in Politics,* Methuen.

OAKESHOTT, M. (1967) 'Learning and teaching', in R.S. PETERS (ed.), *The Concept of Education,* Routledge and Kegan Paul.

O'CONNOR, M. (1979) 'The need to keep ahead of yourself', *Guardian,* 23 October.

OECD (1975) *Report on Educational Development Strategy in England and Wales,* OECD Paris.

OXFORDSHIRE EDUCATION DEPARTMENT (1979) *Starting Points in Self Evaluation.*

PARLETT, M. and HAMILTON, D. (1972) 'Evaluation as illumination' in D. HAMILTON *et al.* (eds), *Beyond the Numbers Game,* Macmillan.

PARLIAMENTARY REPORT (1976) *Tenth Report of the Expenditure Committee on Policy Making in the Deparment of Education and Science,* HMSO.

PEAKER, G. (1979) 'Assessing children's performance', *Special Education,* 2.

PISTON, W. (1970) *Counterpoint,* Gollancz.

PLOWDEN REPORT, THE (1967) *Children and Their Primary Schools,* Central Advisory Council.

POSTER, C. (1976) *School Decision Making,* Heinemann.

PREECE, P. (1980) 'Some problems in the analysis of observational data on the effectiveness of schools', in *Perspectives 1,* Exeter University School of Education.

PRING, R. (1979) 'Confidentiality and the right to know', mimeo, Exeter University School of Education.

PRING, R. (1981) 'Monitoring performance: reflections on the APU', in C. LACEY and D. LAWTON (eds), *Accountability and Evaluation,* Methuen.

PRING, R. and SELBY, C. (1980) *Draft Report on the American Visit,* APU/DES.

QUINTO, F. and MCKENNA, B. (1977) *Alternatives to Standardised Testing,* National Education Association, Washington D.C.

REID, W. (1978) *Thinking about the Curriculum,* Routledge and Kegan Paul.

REID, W. (1979) 'Making the problem fit the method: a review of the "Banbury Enquiry" ', *Journal of Curriculum Studies*, 11, 2.

RENNIE, E. (1980) 'The West Riding screening six years on', *Educational Research*, November.

ROSEN, R.D. (1979) *Psychobabble*, Avon Books, New York.

ROWNTREE, D. (1977) *Assessing Students: How Shall We Know Them?*, Harper and Row.

RUTTER, M., MAUGHAN, B., MORTIMORE, P. and OUSTON, J. (1979) *Fifteen Thousand Hours*, Open Books.

RYLE, G. (1972) 'A rational animal' in R. DEARDEN *et al.* (eds), *Education and the Development of Reason*, Routledge and Kegan Paul.

SCOTTISH COUNCIL FOR RESEARCH IN EDUCATION (1977) *Pupils in Profile*, Hodder and Stoughton.

SCRIVEN, M. (1967) 'The methodology of evaluation' in *Perspectives of Curriculum Evaluation*, AERA Monograph Series on Curriculum Evaluation, 1, Rand McNally.

SCRIVEN, M. (1972) 'Pros and cons about goal-free evaluation', *Evaluation Comment*, December.

SEDDON, G. (1979) 'Sheredes School: examination results summer 1979', mimeo, Sheredes School, Hoddesdon, Hertfordshire.

SHAW, K. (1980) 'Factorial studies, and what they leave out', in *Perspectives 1*, Exeter University School of Education.

SHIPMAN, M. (1979) *In-School Evaluation*, Heinemann.

SIMON, J. (1979) 'What and who is the APU?', *Forum*, autumn.

SIMONS, H. (1980a) 'The evaluative school', *Forum*, spring.

SIMONS, H. (1980b) 'Process evaluation in schools' in C.LACEY and D.LAWTON (eds), *Accountability and Evaluation*, Methuen.

SKILBECK, M. (1980) *Triennial Review 1980–82*, Curriculum Development Centre, Canberra, Australia.

SNIDER, R. (1978) *Back to the Basics?* National Education Association, Washington D.C.

SOCKETT, H. (1980) (ed.) *Accountability in the English Educational System*, Hodder and Stoughton.

SOLTIS, J. (1979) 'Knowledge and the curriculum' in *Teachers College Record*, May.

SPOONER, R.T. (1980) 'Teacher craft', *Education*, 27 June.

STAKE, R. (1967) 'The countenance of educational evaluation' in *Teachers College Record*, July.

STAKE, R. (1976) 'Making school evaluations relevant', *North Central Association Quarterly*, spring.

STAKE, R. (1977) *Evaluating Educational Programmes*, O.E.C.D.

STAKE, R. and EASLEY, J. (1977) *Case Studies in Science Education*, Center for Instructional Research and Curriculum Evaluation, University of Illinois.

STANSBURY, D. (1980) 'The record of personal experience', in T.BURGESS and E. ADAMS (eds), *Outcomes of Education*, Macmillan.

STENHOUSE, L. (1975) *An Introduction to Curriculum Development*, Heinemann.

STENHOUSE, L. (1979) 'The study of samples and the study of cases', presidential address to annual conference of the British Educational Research Association, September.

STENHOUSE, L. (1980) *Curriculum Research and Development in Action*, Heinemann.

STENHOUSE, L. (1981) 'Curriculum research and education process', paper presented to SSRC seminar *Curriculum Research: Agenda for the Eighties*, University of Birmingham, January.

STERNE, M. (1980) 'The Solihull guide for self-evaluation', *Education*, 22 February.

STIBBS, A. (1979) *Assessing Children's Language*, Ward Lock.

STONES, E. (1979) 'The world of APU' in *Forum*, autumn.

STRAUGHAN, R. and WRIGLEY, J. (1980), *Values and Evaluation in Education*, Harper and Row.

STUBBS, M. and DELAMONT, S. (1976) *Explorations in Classroom Observation*, Wiley.

TABA, H. (1962) *Curriculum Development: Theory and Practice*, Harcourt Brace.

TAYLOR, B. (1979) 'Somerset's homegrown yardsticks', *Education*, 21 September.

TAYLOR, W. (1976) 'The head as manager? Some criticisms' in R.S.PETERS (ed.), *The Role of the Head*, Routledge and Kegan Paul.

TAYLOR, W. (1978) *Research and Reform in Teacher Education*, N.F.E.R.

TYLER, R. (1949) *Basic Principles of Curriculum and Instruction*, University of Chicago Press.

TYLER, R., LAPAN, S., MOORE, J., RIVERS, L. and SKIBO, D. (1978) *The Florida Accountability Program: an Evaluation of Its Educational Soundness and Implementation*, National Education Association, Washington D.C.

WARNOCK REPORT, THE (1978) *Special Educational Needs*, H.M.S.O.

WESTBURY, I. (1979) 'Research into classroom processes' in P.H.TAYLOR (ed.) *New Directions in Curriculum Studies*, Falmer Press.

WESTON, P. (1979) *Negotiating the Curriculum: a Study in Secondary Schooling*, N.F.E.R.

WHEELER, D. (1967) *Curriculum Process*, University of London Press.

WILLIAMS, J. (1977) *Learning to Write, or Writing to Learn?* N.F.E.R.

WILLMOTT, A. (1980) Communication to author.

WILSON, C. (1975) *The Craft of the Novel*, Gollancz.

WILSON, J. (1972) *Philosophy and Educational Research*, N.F.E.R.

WOOD, R. (1977) 'Charting the depths of ignorance', *The Times Educational Supplement*, 2 December.

INDEX